W9-CDW-495

The Pocket
Small Business Owner's Guide™ to
Starting Your Business on a Shoestring

The Pocket
Small Business
Owner's Guide™ to
Starting Your
Business on
a Shoestring

Carol Tice

ALLWORTH PRESS
NEW YORK

Allworth Press books may be purchased in bulk at special discounts for sales promotion, corporate gifts, fund-raising, or educational purposes. Special editions can also be created to specifications. For details, contact the Special Sales Department, Allworth Press, 307 West 36th Street, 11th Floor, New York, NY 10018 or info@skyhorsepublishing.com.

17 16 15 14 13   5 4 3 2 1

Published by Allworth Press, an imprint of Skyhorse Publishing, Inc.
307 West 36th Street, 11th Floor, New York, NY 10018.

Allworth Press® is a registered trademark of Skyhorse Publishing, Inc.®, a Delaware corporation.

www.allworth.com

Cover design by Brian Peterson

Library of Congress Cataloging-in-Publication Data is available on file.

ISBN: 978-1-62153-239-2

Printed in the United States of America

Contents

.

Introduction

I once had a good friend come to me all excited because his cousin was going to open an Italian restaurant. He had a great location, an armload of his mother's great Italian recipes, and a fun name: Yo Mama's.

It all sounded wonderful to me. I couldn't wait to go try the cuisine. I followed along eagerly as my friend kept me updated on the restaurant's progress.

Unfortunately, there were delays and more delays. The refrigerator cases took forever to arrive. The contractor who was to install the restaurant booths flaked out. The menus were designed, rejected, and redesigned. Unexpected expenses seemed to crop up at every turn.

What was supposed to be a two-month build-out took six months, while Yo Mama's landlord went right on collecting rent payments. Finally, my friend brought me the sad news— Yo Mama's had closed without ever opening its doors.

My friend's cousin had his entrepreneurial dreams destroyed by the biggest problem afflicting would-be business owners: He overspent and ran out of money.

If what happened to Yo Mama's was a fluke, you wouldn't be reading this. Unfortunately, early death is all too common among business startups. Every year, more than half a million American entrepreneurs start a business, the Small Business Administration (SBA) reports. But many of those businesses don't survive.

SBA data show that three of every ten new businesses close within the first two years. At five years, half the businesses are gone.

Why do these businesses fail? You might chalk it up to management inexperience, inadequate fundraising, or just plain bad luck. But in the end, most businesses close their doors for the same, simple reason Yo Mama's did—because their owners have run out of money.

In nearly twenty years of talking to entrepreneurs and writing about business, I've seen this story repeated over and over. Failure to control expenses means too much cash is going out the door while your business is in its critical, formative months. Overspending starves the business of needed capital, forcing you to borrow and fall into debt. Payments to service that debt starve your cash flow further, which limits your growth options and results in fewer sales. The downward spiral is often irreversible.

Consider this book your practical business survival guide.

Whether you are just thinking about starting a business or have taken the plunge already, this book provides scores of ideas and strategies to help you cut costs and keep your business alive. I've covered how to slash expenses for every aspect of your business, whether you operate a retail, e-commerce, manufacturing, wholesale, or service business.

Many entire books have been written about some of the topics covered here, especially marketing and social-media marketing. My intent with this pocket guide is to give you a basic grounding in the savings opportunities available in *every* aspect of your budding business, all in one handy volume. By providing tips in each area, I'm hoping to help you develop a habit of questioning every expense and looking for free and dirt-cheap alternatives at every turn.

The good news: There has never been a better time to try to start a business on a shoestring. The Internet has brought a wealth of free or cheap resources for entrepreneurs of all stripes. There is also renewed government and charitable interest in supporting and building a thriving small-business sector.

As you build your business, ask yourself: How badly do I want my business to survive? Then, look around and figure out how to cut expenses. The lower your burn rate, the longer you can keep the business alive as it builds to profitability.

If you want the one-line version of what I'll impart in the coming pages, it's this: Every time you're about to spend money on your business, ask yourself if there is a way to avoid, reduce, or postpone this cost. Develop this habit, and it will help set you on the road to business success.

This book is full of real examples of cost-cutting successes and failures culled both from my own experiences running several solopreneur, home-based businesses and from my many years as a business reporter, during which I saw too many good businesses go down in flames. I developed a passion for helping businesses grow and thrive along the way, and I'm excited to present this extensive collection of money-saving ideas for business owners and aspiring entrepreneurs.

I dedicate this book to my parents, Arlene and Bernie Faber, who taught me the value of a dollar.

Carol Tice

Chapter 1

MARKET RESEARCH

If you only read one chapter of this book, this one has the potential to save you the most money.

Why? If you start a business and it turns out that there is no market for what you want to sell, every dollar you spend on the business will be wasted.

It's a common flaw of entrepreneurs that you never think this will happen to you. Your idea is inspired! It's genius! Customers will be lining up around the block, for sure. Or so you think. That's what one new Seattle entrepreneur thought, too, when he started his business in 2010.

The business began when a retired attorney saw a new electric car model that a small engine-maker was introducing to the market. Enchanted by the $11,000 vehicle, the man leased a large storefront on the main drag of his small Seattle town, rolled a couple of the electric cars into the showroom, and waited for the customers to flock. He got a write-up in the local paper. Locals definitely knew he was there.

Three months later, the business had sold exactly zero cars. There were some problems with the car, it turned out. Customers didn't like it much—or not enough to shell out $11,000.

For starters, the car didn't have doors.

It was open on the sides like a golf cart. In the rainy Northwest, no one was going to buy a car without doors. The owner began pressing the manufacturer to add doors to the cars, but the months dragged on, and no doors arrived.

There were other problems, too. The car had a top speed of twenty-five miles an hour, so it could never be driven on busier main streets, much less the freeway. The vehicle could only go twenty miles between charges, so it was only good for short errand runs. These two factors greatly limited the car's appeal.

Finally, there was the price tag, which customers found a bit steep for what was essentially a glorified golf cart. At the same time, some deep-pocketed competition rolled into town—Nissan's all-electric Leaf arrived just a couple of months after this entrepreneur's business opened its doors.

Though the Leaf was more expensive, it had a top speed of ninety miles per hour and a range of one hundred miles between charges. In other words, it was a full-service car. Also, Nissan had gotten the car signed up for federal rebate programs that offered consumers a substantial tax credit for purchasing the vehicle.

It was no surprise when about a year after it opened, the startup electric-car business closed.

"I would have sold any number if I had doors," he sadly told the local paper. But likely, he would have needed much more. This startup's product simply didn't have the features or pricing customers wanted in an electric car.

The competition had a more attractive offering. The company had failed to find out from prospective customers whether they would buy this type of electric car before plunging in to invest and launch the business.

Hopefully, this sad story has sold you on the importance of doing market research before you start your business. If you've started already, it's never too late to adjust course by getting some customer feedback.

MARKET RESEARCH BASICS

The sad tale of the failed electric-car startup provides a cautionary lesson in what can happen when you don't do any market research. To avoid disaster, you need information on four basic areas:

1. **Market competition.** Who already sells this type of product? Who are the market leaders? What market share does each of these competitors currently capture? What are their growth plans?

2. **Customer demand.** What is the overall size of the market for what you want to offer? Is demand projected to grow or shrink in the coming years, and if so by how much?

3. **Needed features.** What options, colors, or sizes do customers want most?

4. **Pricing.** What are customers currently paying for similar products? What would they be
willing to pay for your particular item?

Many business owners avoid doing market research in
part because of the cost—big research firms can charge
thousands to create a custom research report. Fortunately,
you can gather your own market research at little or
no cost.

There are two basic ways to get market research: You can
locate free or affordably priced existing research data, or you
can do your own. The former can get you information on
market size, industry trends, and competitors' offerings and
market share. To find out how customers respond to your
particular product or service, you'll need to do your own
research.

PLACES TO FIND EXISTING MARKET RESEARCH

Unless your business idea is something radically new,
chances are someone has conducted research on your sector
before. You may not be able to get all the details without paying, but you can often get at least some key metrics on the
size and forecasted growth of your sector for free.

Resources for finding free or cheap existing research
include:

- **Press releases.** Visit sites such as PR
  Newswire or PRWeb—or simply use Google's
  News search tab—to search for key terms for

your industry, e.g., "statistics widget industry [current year]." When research firms publish new reports, they often send out a press release that includes some of the key findings. Also watch for free, short, "executive summary" reports that reveal a survey's highlights. Try to discover if there are research firms that focus on your industry, such as Technomic in food service.

- **Competitors.** If your industry has market leaders that dominate the sector, you can bet they are doing market research. Often, you can let the big guys spend the big bucks on research, and simply ride their coattails by borrowing their stats. Watch for new product introduction releases—they may include company research revealing market size, the company's market share in a particular product niche, or customer polls that show demand for particular new models or features. If competitors are publicly traded, watch for call recordings, call transcripts, or slideshow presentations to investors. These will sometimes reveal research on market size and projected growth. Online presentation platforms such as Slideshare may also yield PowerPoint slides loaded with research stats—company executives often forget to take these down after an event.

- **Stock analysts.** If market leaders are publicly traded, check their investor web page for a list of the investment banks and other stock-analysis firms that provide coverage. Then, check these analysts' sites for research reports they have issued, either on the big players or on the sector overall. Analysts with deep experience in their sectors may well have their eyes on privately held players and up-and-comers, too; if so, you can get a lot of hard-to-find intelligence here.

- **Research firms and think tanks.** Independent research firms can be a gold mine of existing research. Increasingly, more of these firms are making some or all of their research available free online rather than distributing it free to clients and charging everyone else a large fee. You may find research houses that look at your industry or even one big competitor in great depth—an example is Directions on Microsoft, which does nothing but analyze the software giant's moves. As with stock analysts, watch for press releases, executive summaries, and presentation slides that reveal research highlights.

- **Trade publications.** Nearly every industry has at least one trade publication that focuses exclusively on the business of that single sector. Examples include *Ad Age* for marketing firms and *Daily Variety* for entertainment-industry executives. (The site TradePub.com lists many trade pubs.) Often, these publications will put out an annual report ranking the top players, which may include figures on industry size, individual companies' annual revenue, or whether competition is growing or shrinking.

- **Industry guides.** In some industries, an organization compiles revenue figures on hundreds of competitors, which often provide their data in exchange for a trade-magazine subscription. Then, these organizations publish all the information supplied by the companies in an annual guidebook. An example is the Chain Store Guides, which cover many sectors of retailing.

- **Trade associations.** Many industry organizations, such as the National Restaurant Association, do regular surveys of their membership and publicly release their findings. These can include top industry trends and forecasts of sector-wide annual sales growth.

- **Industry conventions.** Scan convention schedules from past events to see if survey data was announced in a presentation or keynote session. If so, you may be able to buy a recording of the presentation at little cost, or contact the firm that performed the research work to obtain a copy.

- **Amazon.com.** If you want to know how consumers feel about competing products, read the reviews on Amazon.com or other large e-commerce websites. If consumers feel a product is, for instance, overpriced or of poor quality, they're not shy about sharing. If customer feedback is negative, you may spot problems that suggest a better product you could introduce.

- **Social media.** Another wide-open, free source of customer sentiment is social-media platforms, such as Yelp for restaurants and, especially, Twitter. Many big companies are doing social-media customer care, as cable giant Comcast does with its Twitter account @ComcastCares. Reading big players' customer-service conversations can help you learn about customer frustrations and spot possible opportunities.

- **Your local library.** Most libraries pay for subscriptions to many databases. Your local branch might have a subscription to Hoover's, for instance, which contains sales figures (or estimates) for many private companies.

HOW TO DO YOUR OWN MARKET RESEARCH—THE RIGHT WAY

Once you've gathered all the information you can from available resources, it's time to conduct some market research of your own. Here's how to do your research so that you gain truly valuable customer feedback:

- **Ditch the focus groups.** The problem with focus groups lies in the dynamic of group-think. Often, one or two extroverts quickly dominate the group, squelching opposing opinions and getting everyone to agree with them. You've gathered twelve people together, but you don't end up with twelve opinions. To get good customer feedback, you'll need to talk to people one at a time.

- **Avoid multiple choice.** A common method of market research is to create a survey with multiple-choice answers—with free online tools, such as SurveyMonkey, it's never been easier. The problem is your questions frame the issues and define the possible answers, too. You may not even be asking the right questions, and you'll never know it. If possible, avoid using multiple-choice questionnaires. If you need to use them, make sure to include an "Other" response for each question, with room for a write-in answer. Close with at least one open question such as "What else would you like to tell us about this product?"

- **Don't cheat.** Make sure that your questions don't signal to customers which answer you're hoping they'll give.

  Bad: "Would you pay $9.99 for this?"

  Good: "What would you pay for this?"

- **Encourage dialogue.** Rather than asking questions that can be answered with a simple "yes" or "no," ask open-ended questions that require a more detailed reply. For instance, when Zipcar cofounder Robin Chase was researching names for the car-sharing company in 1999, she carried around index cards with several different names written on them. After briefly explaining that she was starting a company, she'd present her cards and simply say, "What does this suggest to you?" She quickly learned that names with the word "share" in them tested poorly, even though the business idea was a car-sharing company. This led the business to go with the Zipcar name.

Finding Cheap Market Research Help

If you want to gather a lot of customer feedback, it may take too long to do it all yourself. But you don't have to hire a big marketing firm for big money, either. Here are a few ways to get market research assistance at little or no cost:

- **Family and friends.** If you have an extensive network of personal contacts, you might be able to persuade them each to devote an hour or two to surveying prospective customers. Throw them all a pizza party at the end of the day, and you're good.

- **Barter and time banks.** If you have products or services ready to go, you may be able to trade your offering with a marketing professional for research help. Time banks and barter exchanges offer more flexibility. In a nutshell, here is how they work: Members donate their time or services in return for credits on the exchange they can redeem with any other member—the exchange member doesn't have to want what you have to swap. So a member might volunteer to spend an hour taking surveys for you and then choose to get a massage from another member in repayment. Meanwhile, you might pay your debt to the exchange by offering some of your own services to a third member.

- **Marketing, business, and entrepreneurship students.** Business-school teachers are always looking for real-world, hands-on projects or case studies their students can tackle that get them out of the classroom. Contact your local college to see if you could recruit a team of students to do surveys as a class project, for course credit or possibly a small stipend.

- **Student business groups and clubs.** At the high school level and younger, there are organizations that aim to help students acquire entrepreneurship skills. Two of the oldest and best known are Junior Achievement and Future Business Leaders of America. Students involved in these groups are looking to get business experience. Check with your local chapter to see if students would be interested to volunteer or work for a small payment on a marketing project they could present to their group.

Once you start doing market research, your business idea may shift radically as you learn what customers really want. That's what happened to one startup formed during a Stanford University lean startup class in 2011.

Case Study: Autonomow

One team with engineering training wanted to build an automated robotic lawnmower—the Autonomow. But team leader Lee Redden told me that idea was sent back to the drawing board after the team went out and actually talked to their planned target customers, who were golf-course greenskeepers.

"All of them told us they would not buy this thing," he says. "They were really happy with the people they had doing lawnmowing, and it wasn't that expensive."

The Autonomow team began casting about for a more commercial use for their automation technology, and they hit on the idea of building an automated weeder. When they spoke to organic farmers about their idea, they were met with wild enthusiasm, Redden says. Weeding is both expensive and labor-intensive on organic farms, which cannot spray chemicals to kill weeds. The idea for a weeding robot they dubbed the Carrotbot was born.

"The farmers were asking if they could have it *right now*," says Steven Blank, a lean startup expert and Stanford lecturer who cotaught the class. "Any time a customer tries to grab the product out of your hand before it's finished, you've got something."

After hastily assembling a prototype Carrotbot in a single, frantic weekend, the team began testing it with local organic farmers. Based on the farmers' positive response, the team planned to incorporate and seek seed funding to start their business upon graduation.

If the Autonomow team hadn't researched their original idea, they would have wasted energy pursuing a product idea that had no market. Instead, they discovered a true market need and were able to launch a business with a better chance of success.

Chapter 2

BUSINESS PLAN

N ow that you've done some market research and have a sense of who might buy your product or service and at what price, the next step is to create a business plan. What is a business plan? Simply put, it is a description of your business's anticipated future. It describes what you plan to do.

Business plans don't have to be long and complicated. Just a few pages can be a good starting point. If you're looking to pitch your plan to investors in search of funding for your startup, you'll need a more sophisticated plan.

I can just feel your eyes glazing over as I talk about creating this plan. You want to start your business already! But take a moment to check this out, because plunging into business without a plan can be a quick shortcut to overspending.

Writing a business plan will help you map out all the costs of creating and marketing your offering to your target audience. This road map will show you the expenses you need to research to discover actual costs. As you get cost estimates and plug those in, the plan should help you quickly see if your business will make money.

Doing this exercise can help avoid a common startup pitfall—you have a great idea, and your research shows it could sell well, but it turns out to cost more to produce and sell your item than what customers would pay. This is a recipe for failure.

Unless you can raise your prices or cut your expenses, you will lose money steadily until you close your doors. Spotting the lack of profitability early will help you adjust your business model until you have one that produces a profit.

Many books have been written about how to create a business plan. My aim here is to give you a quick grounding in the basics, with a focus on identifying costs and spotting ways to increase profits.

BUSINESS PLAN BASICS

There are three basic parts to a business plan:

- **Concept.** What type of business is this, and what is your game plan for making it successful?

- **Market and marketing.** Who are your customers, where are they, and how do you plan to reach them?

- **Financials.** Before launch, these will be your projections of what your product or service will cost to deliver, the price at which it will sell, and the anticipated units you will sell in a given time period. Later, actual monthly and then quarterly sales and expense figures will replace these projections. Important elements of this section should include an income statement, a cash flow statement, and a balance sheet.

The market research you did previously should help you figure out what to write in those first two parts of the business plan. Now, we'll focus on coming up with financial figures that will help you identify all your costs. This will help you calculate your startup costs and see if you need to find outside funding to launch your business.

If your projections don't show a profit, you have two alternatives: Figure out how to slash costs further, or conclude that this is not a profitable business idea.

I. How to Create an Income Statement

The income statement could be more accurately called an income and expense statement as you will record your income and then deduct all your expenses. The point of this exercise is to figure out the net income of your business—a.k.a. your profit.

You can use the income statement to calculate four basic metrics that help reveal the health and progress of your business. These are:

- Gross margin
- Operating income

- Income before taxes
- Net income

The Formula for Calculating Gross Margin:

net sales (how much revenue your business brings in)

– cost of goods (what you spend to manufacture or purchase any physical products)

= gross margin

Example:

Net sales: $4,000

Cost of goods: $2,500

Gross margin: $1,500, or 37.5 percent

How Is Your Margin? Now that you know your gross margin, the first question is whether this is a healthy figure or a sickly one. Most industries have typical gross margins. These are benchmark figures you want to meet or exceed.

An upscale grocery such as Whole Foods Market, for example, typically enjoys margins around 4 percent, while a more low-end grocery chain, such as Safeway, is lucky to see margins break 1 percent. Meanwhile, Starbucks recently reported operating margins north of 16 percent.

How can you find out what typical margins are in your industry? Try professional associations or organizations. These groups often survey their members and may have hard figures on margins as well as margin trends over time. Trend data can give you an idea of whether your sector is under competitive pressure—you see margins decreasing—or seeing increased opportunity and growing margins.

The Formula for Calculating Operating Income:

gross margin

- operating expenses (a.k.a. selling, general and administrative costs, this category also includes the loss you show from the shrinking value of your equipment over time, or depreciation, and the cost of such things as office supplies, labor, rent, and marketing)

= operating income

Example:

Gross margin: $1,500

Operating expenses: $850

Operating income: $650

Are You Running Your Business . . . into the Ground? If you see a negative number at this point, operating expenses are too high. It's time to examine your overhead and see where you could cut back. Your business might need to find a cheaper rental space or scale back that marketing campaign.

The Formula for Calculating Pretax Income:

operating income

– interest expenses on loans and other debts

= pretax income

Example:

Operating income: $650

Interest payments: $100

Pretax income: $550

Drowning in Debt? If you've had a positive figure until this point but now you see red ink, your business is probably overleveraged. Servicing your debt is keeping you from making a profit. Examine ways to reorganize or pay off debt to cut interest payments down.

The Formula for Calculating Net Income:

pretax income

– income taxes owed

= net income

Example:

Pretax income: $550

Income taxes owed: $150

Net income: $400

Here it is, folks. If you've heard business owners refer to "the bottom line," net income is what they're talking about—the final entry on your income statement. Net income is the money your business makes after all expenses.

In the case of my example, the business made $4,000 in sales and net income is 10 percent of that, or $400. In some business types that would be considered a great result, in others a disaster. For instance, if you had an online-only business exclusively selling digital products with a very low cost of overhead or production, you'd expect profits to be much higher. If you own a grocery store, its net income would likely be lower.

Often, in a startup, you'll see a negative net income figure at first. What's important is the trend, though. You want to see net income progressing rapidly toward the breakeven point (where net income would be zero) and from there to profitability.

You may wonder why you should take the time to break out income and costs in this elaborate way. Why not just add up all the expenses and find the net income? This breakout allows you to see each element and spot where costs are draining your profits away.

II. How to Create a Cash Flow Statement

The cash flow statement will help you understand what is happening to the money your business makes over time. The statement starts and ends with two key figures for both the current and most recent previous period:

- Net receipts (revenue from selling your products or services in this period)

- Net cash flow (the amount of cash left at the end of the period, after all types of income and expenses have been considered)

These two figures will rarely be identical. The cash flow statement analyzes income and expenditures for three aspects of the business: operations, investing, and financing.

Examples of Items That Increase Net Cash:

- Interest or dividends paid on company investments

- Profits from stock sales

- Cash realized from selling company assets, such as equipment or trucks

- A reduction in merchandise inventory (leaves more cash on hand relative to the previous period)

Examples of Items That Reduce Net Cash:

- Payouts or dividends paid to owners or shareholders

- Debt payments

- Rent or lease payments

- Property or equipment acquisitions

- An increase in merchandise inventory (drains more cash compared to the previous period)

The cash flow statement ends with two figures, showing the amount of net cash at the end of the previous and current periods. Hopefully, over time you will see net cash growing. The cash flow statement can also help you spot costs that are draining the company of cash.

Sometimes, it's necessary to spend more cash to grow your business—for instance, you might purchase more merchandise for a busy holiday season but not realize the additional income until the following period. This is why many big businesses like to compare their performance to the same period a year earlier, when seasonal issues were similar.

Some of the key figures in a cash flow statement are comparative numbers that show how a figure has changed from the previous period, usually a month or a quarter. A simple monthly cash flow statement might look like this:

Income (expense) from operations:

Net receipts:	$ 103,000
Additions to cash:	
Decrease in accounts receivable:	$ 15,000
Subtractions to cash:	
Increase in inventory:	($ 42,000)
Net cash from operations:	$ 76,000

Income (expense) from investing:

Equipment purchase:	($ 23,000)

Income (expense) from financing:

Loan payment:	($ 2,000)

Net cash flow: $ 51,000

The cash flow statement provides a snapshot of the money that came into and went out of the business during that period. To see the bigger picture of how your business is faring, you need to create a balance sheet.

III. How to Create a Balance Sheet

Now that you have an income statement and a cash flow statement, you're ready to sum it all up on the balance sheet.

Your balance sheet tells the story of whether your business is operating profitably—in other words, whether it's growing in value or declining. It is a statement of assets, liabilities (fancy accountingspeak for debts), and owner equity. The liabilities are subtracted from the assets to show the current value of the business to its owners.

Your business assets may include:

- Cash on hand

- Investments such as certificates of deposit

- The value of merchandise inventory

- The value of equipment or real estate

- Accounts receivable—money customers owe but have not yet paid

- Any anticipated tax refund

Liabilities might include:

- Payments owed on any loans or outstanding credit lines

- Anticipated income taxes

- Lease payments owed for property or equipment

- Accounts payable—what your business owes vendors for merchandise and services

The difference between your assets and your liabilities is considered the equity of your business, or its value. If you have shareholders in your business, it is the shareholders' equity—the positive balance would be divided by the number of shares to arrive at a per-share value. If there is a negative balance, then shareholders have negative equity, and their shares do not currently have resale value.

A startup business's balance sheet might look like this:

Balance sheet for quarter ended 3/13:
Assets:
Cash:	$ 23,000
Inventory:	$ 35,000
Accounts receivable:	$ 5,000
Equipment:	$ 12,000
Total assets:	**$ 75,000**

Liabilities:
Labor costs owed:	$ 24,000
Equipment rental:	$ 11,200
Marketing campaign:	$ 9,000
Accounts payable:	$ 3,000
Office rental:	$ 3,500
Loan payments:	$ 9,500
Est. taxes owed:	$ 21,000
Total liabilities:	**$ 81,200**

Shareholder equity:	**($ 6,200)**
Total liabilities plus shareholder equity:	**$ 75,000**

The key thing to know here—the balance sheet is called that because it is supposed to balance out. Assets must equal liabilities plus shareholder equity. If liabilities exceed assets as in the example above, the negative shareholder equity balances it out. In this example, assets exceed liabilities by $6,200. The business is not yet at breakeven and has a negative market value. As the business begins to bring in more cash, the balance sheet will improve, giving the owners a valuable asset.

Figuring ROI

One of the useful things to do with a balance sheet is to see whether you are getting a good return on investment (ROI) with the money you put into the business. Your goal should be to get a better return on your invested money in your business than you would have received if you had simply put it into a traditional, low-risk investment vehicle such as a money-market fund or certificate of deposit.

For instance, if banks are paying 3 percent interest, you'd want to see substantially more than that—let's say at least a 7 percent return, but hopefully much more—coming from your business. Why more? Running a business is far more risky than putting money into a certificate of deposit, so the return should be better as well.

The big value of your balance sheet isn't as a one-time snapshot, but in watching how this sheet changes over time. As your business grows, you want to see net assets growing and black ink on that bottom line, not red.

Example: You put $10,000 into the business initially. At the end of the first year, you see your balance sheet shows assets have grown to $12,000. Pat yourself on the back! Subtracting your original $10,000 investment, you have $2,000 in profit, a 20 percent annual return on your money.

The "Plain Vanilla" Business Plan Shortcut

One of the easiest ways to create the financials for a business plan is to use the existing financial statements of a business similar to yours. You might think it would be difficult to get business owners to share their profit and loss figures with you, but there is one way to ask for this information that's often successful.

Make friends with business owners in your industry who operate in a different market and are not your competitors. Then, ask if you could possibly see a "plain vanilla" copy of their business plans. That's a copy with all the budget lines for income and costs in their profit and loss statements—*with all the figures erased.* Since this doesn't reveal much about how their business is doing, many owners are willing to provide this blank budget.

This helps you by providing a guide to all of the budget items your business type will have. It's a common mistake when you're starting a new business that you don't consider all of the required costs . . . because *you don't know what they are yet.* Catching a look at another entrepreneur's budget will help avoid this problem.

You might also ask some basic financial questions that can be answered without revealing exact figures, such as "What is your cost of labor as a percent of sales?" The answers will give you more clues as to the cost levels you should expect without forcing the owner to divulge his exact finances.

If you can't get a small business owner to share figures, another approach is to look at the financial statements of a publicly traded company in your sector. Public companies must file their financials with the Securities and Exchange Commission (SEC), and you can read them on the SEC website charmingly known as Edgar. Obviously, this type of business will be much larger than yours, and so may have economies of scale your startup will not enjoy. But you can still get a sense of the major costs in your type of business from reviewing it.

Keep Updating

A business plan shouldn't be something you write and then stick in a drawer. Consider it a living document you will change and add to as your business idea evolves. When you open for business, begin replacing projections with real figures. Adjust your plan accordingly to make sure your business is still on the path to profit.

At any major milestone—you add a new product, hire a new manager, prepare to seek financing, or sense a change in industry trends—your plan should change, too.

Business Plan Help

The Small Business Administration has a guide for learning how to write a business plan. You can also get free sample business plans at Bplans.com.

Chapter 3

TRAINING

M any entrepreneurs get a business idea that springs from their skills and work experience. But sometimes, you want to dive into a new field with your business.

If you need to learn new skills, you can often find a way without investing thousands of dollars or getting a four-year degree. Here are a few avenues for low-cost or free training:

JOB SHADOWING

Franchisors know that one of the best ways to learn a business is to work in one. That's why they often provide that opportunity to new franchisees during their training.

If you're not part of a franchise system, that's OK—you can put together your own job-shadowing training program. Just identify a similar business near you (but not so close that you'd be in direct competition). Approach the owner, and tell her you're interested in learning this type of business and willing to volunteer your time. See if she'd be willing to have your free help for a week or two, or even longer. She may just jump at the chance.

The best thing about doing job shadowing is that it provides a reality check on whether the type of business you dream of opening is really suited to your talents and interests. Many entrepreneurs think of operating a quick-serve restaurant, which they imagine could be a cash machine without requiring much on-site time from them. A week behind the counter at a Subway will cure you of these notions. Any type of retail store runs best when owners are frequently on site. Don't like standing on your feet ten hours a day or dealing with low-wage help who may not speak English well? You will find out fast that this is not the business for you—and discovering that early could save you a fortune.

Likewise, a business providing home health care to seniors consists mostly of making cold sales calls. Drive around with a health-care business owner for a day and see if you could imagine yourself doing that, week in and week out. You'll also get a front-row seat on the sales angles that work in that business sector.

If you can't job shadow, see if you could simply take a local owner to a nice lunch and ask him about his business. How many hours does he put in? What does he like best and least about the work? Would he open the business today if he had it to do over, knowing what he knows now? Sometimes a business may seem successful on the outside, but if you dig deeper, you uncover a less rosy picture.

Don't forget to ask the owner how he learned his trade. He may point you to more training resources.

APPRENTICESHIP

If you don't want to volunteer your time, consider serving a formal apprenticeship. During many apprenticeships, you'll be paid a modest hourly wage to learn on the job.

Many people are familiar with apprenticeship programs for classic building trades, such as electrical or plumbing contracting, but in fact formal apprenticeships are widely available in more than 1,000 fields. Some of the more unusual skills you can learn as an apprentice include:

- Arson investigation
- Beekeeping
- Dry cleaning
- Glass blowing
- Horse training
- Swimming-pool servicing
- Tree surgery

Apprenticeships are regulated by the US Department of Labor's Office of Apprenticeship, which has criteria that employers must follow to run a formal apprenticeship program. There are also many unofficial apprenticeship opportunities, but they may be unpaid or not as rigorous in imparting the needed skills.

The key thing to know about formal apprenticeships is that they are usually lengthy—from one to four years. You may or may not want to invest the time required to learn the skills you need in this way. But if you do, you'll get a chance to spend a lot of time up close with a business owner in your chosen field, earning while you learn.

The best way to connect with apprenticeships in your area is to contact the Apprenticeship Office for your state.

Of course, there are shorter, more informal apprenticeships entrepreneurs create on their own. Here's the story of how one young entrepreneur used a casual apprenticeship to start his business:

Case Study: America's Swimming Pool Co.

When Stewart Vernon was getting ready to graduate from the College of Charleston in South Carolina in 2002, he knew just one thing about his future: He didn't want to get a job. He wanted to start a business. Networking in the local business community in his hometown of Macon, Georgia, he struck up a conversation with a banker and an older entrepreneur who were looking to back a new startup.

The pair had noticed that there weren't a lot of swimming-pool maintenance companies in town and that one of the primary companies was run by an elderly man who would probably soon retire. They wanted Vernon to research the opportunity with the idea that he might be the operating partner of a business they would back financially.

Vernon spent six months researching the idea and found there was room in the marketplace for another pool-maintenance firm. He approached the elderly pool man and learned he was indeed preparing to retire. Vernon created a business plan and presented it, but the banker and entrepreneur got cold feet, deciding they'd like to partner with a more experienced business owner.

"I remember sitting on my kitchen floor staring with the phone in my hand," Stewart says. "I hung up, and I was just devastated."

After thinking about the problem overnight, though, Vernon realized that there was nothing stopping him from starting a pool business on his own. But the clock was ticking: the prime summer season was approaching, and Vernon needed to learn the business fast, so he could start up in time to line up new customers during the busy season.

He asked the retiring pool man if he could learn the business by working with him at no charge. It turned out the gentleman was hoping to find someone who would take care of his few remaining customers, so he agreed.

For two months that spring, Vernon arose early and drove to a local Burger King parking lot, where he'd leave his car and get into the veteran pool man's truck. After a few days of watching, Vernon began to slowly take over some of the pool maintenance tasks. The days were long, as the elderly Southern gentleman liked to shoot the breeze with his clients and take his time. Usually, it was past dark by the time Vernon returned to his car.

"I worked incredibly hard, long hours, and it was so valuable to learn how a pro did this," he recalls. "I learned it didn't matter if we had to stop a job and go get a different piece of equipment—the decisions were always based on customers' needs."

In the course of the apprenticeship, the pool man moved into a more active mentorship role, taking Vernon to buy tools and introducing him to pool-supply vendors. By summer, Vernon was ready to strike out on his own and started his business with the old man's eight remaining clients.

That first year, Vernon brought in $70,000. "Once I took over, it grew organically from word of mouth," he says. "I did door-to-door sales, too." From a single-man operation that first year, Vernon went on to grow America's Swimming Pool Co. to $1 million in sales in 2004. He later franchised the business, which today has nearly 100 locations and roughly $15 million in system-wide sales.

TRADE, TECHNICAL, AND COMMUNITY COLLEGES

Depending on what sort of business you'd like to open, there may be a trade, technical, or community college program where you could learn the skills you need quickly and affordably. Technical colleges offer programs in practical skills in areas such as:

- Advertising and media

- Automotive repair

- Building design, construction, and maintenance

- Business finance and administration

- Computers

- Culinary training

- Electronics

- Fashion design and marketing

- Internet-based business

- Legal fields

- Medical billing

- Aviation

- Cosmetology

- Floral design

- Travel

These courses can be a great way to pick up new skills in a business specialty. You can find a trade-tech school near you through the Association for Career and Technical Education.

Don't have time to leave your business to study? Consider online universities. Virtual colleges have exploded over the past decade, offering a boggling array of classes. Before signing up, investigate the accreditation of the institution—there are plenty of scams on the Internet that offer low-value courses at high prices. You can check credentials at the US Department of Education Accreditation website.

Be sure to investigate scholarship programs that may be available through your chosen college or school, as well as independent scholarships that might cut your education costs.

QUICKIE IN-PERSON COURSES

If you don't have time to sign onto a one- or two-year or longer college training program, investigate your local college's extension program. For instance, when I got into journalism, I was already working editing a weekly newspaper and didn't have time to go back to school full time.

The solution? I signed up for journalism classes through UCLA Extension. The courses were just a couple of hundred dollars each and held at night, when I had the time to attend.

Many business skills are taught through independent adult-education providers, such as The Learning Annex, which now offers a range of in-person and online classes that cost as little as 99 cents. Take a look at what's taught through your local Parks & Recreation department, too—often, there is a wide range of affordable courses.

ONLINE LEARNING

Accredited universities are not the only place to get training. The Internet has enabled knowledgeable professionals in many fields to create their own web-based learning platforms. Some of these have strong reputations for quality, while others are useless junk—so do your research and be discerning.

An example of a valuable resource is the Lynda Online Tutorials site, which offers thousands of software training videos. Founded by Lynda Weinman, Lynda.com's training offer—you can watch all the videos you want on the site for just $25 a month—is an example of the sort of low-cost, quality training you can find online. More than forty-five million people use Lynda.com in a typical year, *Wired* magazine reported.

Sometimes, a simple Google search may turn up a free training video you can watch or a blog post you can read to learn what you need. Rather than using the paid-membership model, some training platforms work on an advertising-based income model—the trainings are free to you, and advertisers pay to put their message in front of the site's large audience. An example is W3Schools, which offers thousands of free tech- and web-skills trainings. The site had 1.2 billion page views in 2011.

Since these are unaccredited online education sources, be sure to research thoroughly before signing up. Ask other professionals in the industry if they think a certain educator provides valuable information and—if it is a paid training—if the value of that training is good. Search chat forums for negative feedback, and ask around your own networks to make sure an online instructor is providing current, valuable information at a fair price.

BOOKS AND E-BOOKS

If you want to learn a skill that could be learned from a book, let the enormous catalog at Amazon.com be your guide. Enter key words in their "book" search menu, and sort it by relevance or by most recent items to get the most updated trainings. With the rise in popularity of its Kindle tablet reader, Amazon is growing its Kindle e-book offerings, too.

Remember that e-books are often self-published and haven't been through an editorial process, so investigate the author's credentials and check out the reviews before you buy.

BASIC BUSINESS TRAINING

Finally, there is one skill set all new business owners need. If this is your first business endeavor, invest in some basic classes in how to operate a business—it will be money well spent. Community colleges often offer these, and the Small Business Administration has resources in this area, too.

Chapter 4

E-Commerce

Using an e-commerce website as your business's initial launchpad is a great way to keep startup costs down. Whether you consider your website primarily a place to do testing and market research on your concept before opening a brick-and-mortar store or you plan to make e-commerce your only sales channel, you can't go wrong starting here because it's so inexpensive.

The rise of Internet business is both a blessing and a curse. It's never been easier to start a business with the change you found in your couch cushions . . . but it's equally easy for everyone else to do it, too.

The mysteries of pricing are gone now—a quick Google search, and your customers know exactly what all your competitors are charging for the same item. The barriers to entry in business have fallen, so it takes a little creativity to discover an online business niche where you can stand out from the crowd and still sell items at a decent profit.

Getting off the ground online, though, can be done on a teenager's babysitting money now. The e-commerce site

AppSumo, for instance, was famously started in 2010 for $60 and with a reported two hours of (outsourced) work. The startup went like this:

Founder Noah Kagan, a former Facebook staffer, had the idea of doing a Groupon for Nerds site—a place that would offer discounts on technology and information products that help online entrepreneurs. First, a bare-bones version of the site was built with Third World outsourced coding labor.

Then, Kagan placed a cheap ad on the bookmarking site Reddit—heavily favored by techies—with Appsumo's first discount deal, to see if anyone would buy it. After the deal was a wild success, that income was used to continue improving the site.

Today's AppSumo is a solid success and employs a staff of fifteen, selling scores of tools and training courses in a dozen different business areas, from online advertising strategies to using WordPress.

E-COMMERCE BUSINESS TOOLS:
THE FREE AND THE CHEAP

If you found that little tale inspiring, here's a rundown on some of the tools you might use to launch an Internet business and how to get everything for free or near to it. Many of these recommendations come from Seattle-area business consultant Annette Walker of Seattle mobile-marketing firm Astonish Inc.

- **Web hosting.** Start with a free host, such as VSTORE, or go pro right away with a paid host for $50 or less per year. Or, if you're reselling others' goods or selling your own handmade crafts, you might simply set up a store on eBay or Etsy. Take advantage of the portals' massive traffic to attract buyers, and pay a small commission with customers' money once you start making sales.

- **Web design.** Some e-commerce web hosts offer package deals for design along with web hosting, and many more offer free trials. Other cost-conscious entrepreneurs barter for these services, hire a web-savvy teen, or outsource them abroad.

- **Key word analysis.** There are paid tools, too, but the free Google Keyword Analytics tool provides a good start in determining what phrases you want your site to rank highly for on search. Other useful free options include KeywordSpy and SEMRush.

- **Search engine optimization (SEO) tools.** Depending on the platform on which you build your e-commerce business, there is an array of free and cheap tools available to help you optimize your site to rank highly in search results, and many free-trial offers. For instance, SEOMOZ offers a thirty-day trial of its suite of SEO management tools, and for bloggers, Copyblogger's Scribe SEO tool has plans that start at $17 a month.

- **Word processing.** Instead of a pricey Microsoft Office suite, try Apache Open Office or Libre Office and Google Docs, says Walker.

- **Email.** Ditch your Microsoft Office Outlook program and use free Gmail as your interface, recommends Walker.

- **Email marketing program.** Mailchimp is free up to your first 2,000 subscribers—plenty of opportunity to build income there before you have to pay anything.

- **Telecommunications.** Walker likes Grasshopper, which enables your virtual team to seem like it's based in one office from clients' point of view while really operating on cell phones around the globe.

- **Mobile marketing.** Walker says she uses Twilio's OpenVBX service, which enables you to establish a company phone number that can be answered by any sort of device anywhere— a traditional phone, team member's smartphone, or computer VOIP, such as Skype.

- **Calendar/appointment planning.** Walker uses Google Calendar, which is easy to share with business partners.

- **Wikis for collaboration.** Free Google web pages can serve as wiki pages to build "institutional memory" in a virtual team, notes Walker.

- **Invoicing.** SimpleInvoices is among the providers of entirely free invoicing, and other, more robust platforms, such as Freshbooks, have a free trial for your first few clients.

- **Business management.** Free comprehensive small-business platforms, such as SohoOS, provide free invoices, payment tracking, inventory management, and more.

- **Idea tracking.** Free Evernote is a widely popular tool in this category.

- **Graphics.** There are a ton of free graphics online on many sites, such as FreeGraphics. org. Can't find what you want? Hire a teenage student from a local high school or college digital-design course.

- **Photos.** Free images are readily available on many sites, including Flickr Creative Commons, MorgueFile, and FreeDigitalPhotos. In some cases, you must include an attribution link giving the photographer credit.

- **Photo editing and screen capture**. Jing offers a free alternative to pricier editing and screencasting software.

- **Software development.** Free version-control sites, such as GitHub, enable virtual teams to collaborate without confusion over which is the most current version of a document, says Walker.

- **Incorporating.** Save a bundle on lawyers through sites such as MyCorporation.com, which will help you handle the paperwork for starting your business for $100 or less.

Eleven Ways to Earn Money from Your Website

While it may seem the Internet is a Wild West of untamed earning opportunity, in fact there are a fairly limited number of ways you can make money from your site. While there are always new twists emerging, here is a look at the basic options in website earnings:

- **Physical products.** These might be items you manufacture or buy wholesale and resell as a "drop shipper," never touching the goods but simply directing the distributor to send the order directly to your customer.

- **Digital products.** One of the highest margin online selling opportunities is creating your own e-books or courses. Once you've created the product, delivery takes a single click, and operating costs are low.

- **Consulting, teaching, or training.** Many experts and consultants make their major coin selling their online courses or offering in-person or online small-group or one-on-one coaching.

- **Affiliate selling.** One of the most popular and lucrative forms of online selling, affiliate selling involves promoting the products and services of others and then earning a commission for sending your customers to that seller. Fifty percent commissions are common in some industries.

- **Ad sales.** Some sites sell banner ads to just one or a few advertisers, while others post many ads. You might sell ads at a flat monthly fee, or take a small commission on sales made through your ad. Google Adsense advertising—one of the most popular types of commission-sales advertising—is a common example of this approach. These ads may display as sidebar boxes or as a line of text that interrupts an article or blog post. Other sites earn from text-link ads, which link key words in articles to sales offers.

- **Public speaking.** Many of the top-earning website operators use their blogs or websites to build their authority and online reputation and then leverage that to land highly paid public speaking gigs at trade shows and conventions.

- **Contests.** Much like the old Publishers Clearing House sweepstakes, some sites make money by offering products or services to contest winners and collecting a fee for each entry.

- **Sponsorships.** If your site attracts a large audience in a particular demographic, you may be able to attract corporate sponsors. For instance, inspirational writer Stephanie Nielson of the blog *NieNie Dialogues* has corporate sponsors recently including Seagram's and American Express.

- **Paid writing gigs.** Many successful bloggers end up getting offered paid writing gigs from blog posts to newspaper columns to book contracts.

- **Merchandising.** If your site develops a distinctive brand, you might sell T-shirts, mugs, and other materials bearing your logo.

- **Services.** Some websites provide services to readers and earn money through this—for instance, ProBlogger runs a job board on which companies pay to list their ads seeking bloggers.

Many of these strategies, particularly those reliant on selling through ads, are generally not very successful until you have built a fairly large audience. The advantage of selling your own physical and digital products is that you can begin making sales fairly soon.

There are several drawbacks to ad-based sales strategies to consider before plunging ahead in that direction. First, ads are a turnoff for many website visitors, so if you deploy ads too early, before building a substantial following, you may merely drive viewers away. As Internet visitors grow savvier, sites plastered with ads are harder and harder to use to build an audience, as customers know there are clean, ad-free sites they can visit instead.

Second, ads generally lead to someone else's website, where the customer then makes the sale. So you're sending customers away from your own site and dissipating their loyalty to your own brand while only making a percent of that sale.

Finally, many ad networks that automatically serve ads may present ads your audience could find inappropriate or even offensive. So sign up for these programs with caution and test them carefully with your audience. Many site owners sign up individual advertisers themselves so they can be more certain about what sort of ads will appear on their sites.

CASE STUDY: HOUSE OF RAVE

Neville Medhora started his first business, House of Rave, in 2001 when he was a seventeen-year-old high school student. He built the site, which sells glow sticks and other party supplies, on his high school's computers because, he explains, their computers and Internet offered faster processing speeds than his home setup.

He had researched the niche and found there were only a couple of competitors selling these products at the time, and their websites weren't very attractive.

"I spent about $200 on a merchant account," he says. "I was using free hosting. It was very 'ghetto.'"

At first, Medhora thought the audience for his products would be teenagers who attend floating parties known as raves (hence the name). But he quickly learned that this young audience didn't have much disposable cash. He began targeting party planners instead.

His first order came within the first month, for $54 worth of merchandise. He emailed the order off to the vendor, who shipped the supplies directly to the customer. Medhora had smartly negotiated for terms of net thirty days from the vendor, so his $54 from the customer's credit card transaction cleared well before the bill arrived, allowing him to pay for the goods with the customer's money. He netted $30.

He landed one of his key vendors with a bold strategy—he swiped the manufacturer's photos from their website and installed them on House of Rave. He then showed the vendor how much better his site looked, and proposed that they let him set up a retail account. His better-designed site quickly began outselling the manufacturer's website, and Medhora soon expanded to sell this vendor's entire merchandise line.

"A lot of people approach a vendor and say, 'I'm thinking about starting a store online—what do I do, by the way?'" Medhora says. By showing the supplier his site was ready to roll and looked professional—and neglecting to mention his age—Medhora says he made a good impression and was able to bring the vendor on board to help his business.

For a primer on ways to market your e-commerce business, see the online-marketing sections of the following chapters on Sales, Advertising, and Marketing.

Chapter 5

SALES

I t's been said that nothing happens in a business until somebody sells something. And this old saw is still around because it is simply true.

Selling is the core activity of every successful business, no matter if you're going into e-commerce, opening a store, or offering consultations. But when you're starting out, you often don't have the budget to hire a seasoned, six-figure sales manager and a team of crack sales staff to go out and sell your product or service.

Fortunately, there are many ways to stimulate sales at little cost. Here's a look at some diverse shoestring approaches to selling.

DO IT YOURSELF

Many startup entrepreneurs are their companies' first—and often best—salespersons. After all, nobody knows their product or service better. When Brad Gruno started his now-successful raw-snack company, Brad's Raw Chips, he says he outsourced or delegated other tasks to leave him more time to make sales calls himself to health food stores.

"I was good at it because I was passionate about the product," Gruno recalls. "I ate it and lost weight. I was my best spokesperson."

Make Your Website Sell

Many new businesses in the twenty-first century won't be hiring any salespeople, and the owners won't be knocking themselves out selling, either. This is because their website is their primary sales tool. A well-designed website can be your 24/7 sales assistant, ringing up sales while you sleep, eat, vacation, and otherwise enjoy life.

Most e-commerce websites don't do all they could to serve as a strong sales tool, though. Here is a crash course in the basics of an effective e-commerce site:

- **Optimize for SEO.** Do keyword research to discover the best search terms to attract buyers to your type of site. Ideal for most niche e-commerce businesses are terms that don't get huge numbers of searches but get decent traffic and are less competitive. Then, get those words into your header, tagline, and metatags. Use those phrases as you compose your copy (but not too often, or Google will think it's a spammy site). Turn your site into an inbound marketing engine with the power to get customers to your site and complete the sale without you.

- **Choose a clean, uncluttered design.** I've reviewed hundreds of websites for solopreneurs, and if they make one common mistake, it's that most are too busy. Eliminate the flashing ads, drop-down menus, double rows of tabs, and multiple sidebars. Make sure your typeface is big and easily readable.

- **Pass the three-second test.** Studies have shown that many site visitors take just a few seconds to look around before deciding to stay or leave. Make it clear at a quick glance what your site sells, so that customers don't depart.

- **Pass the no-header test.** Make sure your navigation tabs tell the story of what you sell as well. A bunch of generic tabs such as "About," "Products," and "Services" don't reveal much about what you do. Instead, say "Real estate consulting" or "Toys." Visitors should be able to look at your tabs and tell what you do, even if they skim past the header.

- **Limit the choices.** Each page of your site should have just one main purpose. Maybe it's to get visitors to join your mailing list.

Maybe it's to sell them a particular product. Whatever the goal, don't have a long list of options, as it just confuses visitors. When readers are confused, they tend to take no action and leave.

- **Provide information.** The information customers need to make a purchase should be easy to find. If you have complex products and services, create FAQ pages or long sales pages that give all the details.

- **Be easy to reach.** One of the most common mistakes I see on business websites is missing contact information. Many online shoppers are wary of sites where there is no phone number or street address. So reassure customers you're legit with prominently posted and complete contact information. The best place to put your contacts is at the top of your website, where it's visible on every page. Don't make customers click through to a "Contact" page—or supply only a fill-in email form on that page, where customers can't even learn your email address. Remember that every click prospects must make represents a "pushback" point at which they might give up and leave. If your products or services are particularly complex, consider creating a "live chat" feature through which customers can get quick answers.

Customer Referrals

Turn your customers into a low-cost sales force by asking them to refer your business. You can get customers more interested by offering a small finder's fee for referrals.

For a retailer, this fee might take the form of a $20-off coupon. I know a commercial real estate property manager who pays $200 to each broker who brings him a client. Either way, these referral payments are chump change compared to hiring full-time sales employees.

You can also "pay" referring customers with merchandise or services rather than cash. Since these cost you less than the customer pays at retail, you can deliver more value to the customer while spending less out of pocket.

To stimulate more referrals from your customers, be sure to recognize their effort, especially if you are not paying. A quick phone call or note lets customers know you appreciate that they're talking you up to their friends—and keeps them sending you more referrals.

If you think you have customers who might repeatedly refer you, consider a graduated rewards plan. That way, if someone refers five or ten customers to you in the course of a year, that referrer would receive bigger rewards per referral than people who sent just one new customer.

You might be surprised at the enthusiasm with which your customers greet an offer of referral payments, especially if they are substantial. A certain segment of the population views referrals as a meaningful source of income. These are most often students or retirees who could use extra cash.

When my husband sold Toyotas, he reported to me that several retired/disabled longtime customers sent his company at least one or two customers monthly in order to get the $100 referral fee. These customers loved Toyotas and saw referring car purchasers as a great opportunity to supplement their monthly income.

Consider doing something special on top of your ordinary bonus for these frequent referrers. Take your top referrer out to dinner each year—then, write about it in the company's marketing emails that go out to other customers to promote your referral program.

Affiliate Sales

Many e-commerce sites use an affiliate-sales approach, signing up hundreds of other website owners who will advertise or mention their products. This can greatly increase the "reach" of your company and bring you new customers you might never have found on your own.

You pay only if an affiliate sends you a customer who actually makes a purchase. Affiliate fees are set by you, with many businesses offering 20 percent to 50 percent. Affiliate programs are highly customizable, so you could offer commissions only on certain products, or only for a set length of time, or pay higher-volume affiliates a bigger cut. This allows you to control when you pay commissions and how much you are willing to spend to pay affiliates.

The costs of setting up an affiliate sales program are fairly minimal. For instance, I paid $99 for the software I use that tracks affiliate payments for people who sell memberships to my freelance writers' community. From there, it's a matter of creating promotional materials for your affiliates—graphical banners and text ads the affiliates can use on their sites and in social media.

Commission-Only Salespeople

Often, in a down economy, cash-strapped companies will use this pay structure to bring on more sales staff. You pay no salary and only pay based on sales volume.

Commissions can be high, but you only pay sales staffers from customers' money paid when they make purchases. This makes commission-only payments a great way to ensure you don't run into cash flow problems in paying your sales staff.

Independent Product Reps

Save the overhead of hiring a full-time salesperson by using independent reps. These salespeople often represent multiple products in an industry and use their connections to help you make sales. Employing indie reps can be a way to get a highly trained sales force you can afford, because they are only working for you part time.

A drawback here is that indie reps are not as focused on your one offering as staff salespeople will be, but reps can get your product in front of major chains and other big clients. You can also easily expand or change the territories you want to sell in by adding more reps in new regions or dropping reps who aren't performing.

To successfully recruit good independent reps, you'll need to have your sales process well organized. Product spec sheets, sample sales letters, sales scripts for phone calls, and the like should all be ready to go. You'll also need a sales management system such as Salesforce.com for tracking your reps' leads and making sure the reps get credit for their sales.

Commission levels for indie reps vary widely. Be sure to research norms in your industry for paying independent reps so that you provide a competitive payment structure but don't overpay.

Relationship-Based Selling

If there are complementary businesses you could band together with to drive sales, this can be a great way to grow the business without spending out of pocket. This is the strategy used by Lisa Hufford, who founded Simplicity Consulting in Kirkland, Washington, in 2006. An experienced former Microsoft sales director, Hufford went into consulting to afford herself more family time.

Rather than simply selling her own consulting, she made her company a hub for similar consultants. All of the other consultants involved in this sales partnership served like free salespeople, talking up Simplicity Consulting to prospective clients in hopes of also getting consulting work through the company.

This setup allowed the consultants to collaborate and share referrals. The result was that revenue at the company soared from $300,000 to $11.5 million within three years, the business newsletter *RainToday* reported.

Make Everyone a Salesperson

In a startup, every person should be trained in how to answer the phone or respond to emails and close sales. If your receptionist or website administrator can also sell, it helps postpone the day when you need to hire a full-time, dedicated salesperson.

Train all employees to be knowledgeable on your offering's features and benefits so they can discuss them if they get a customer on the phone or strolling into the office. Then, teach them to ask for the sale.

If you have a cash register, everyone should know how it works. If you have order sheets that need filling out, make sure everyone can do that. All employees should go through your sales training process, if you have established one, so they all know how to sell and understand what salespeople are up against when they go out to sell.

Treat Sellers Like Kings and Queens

Whatever type of sales help you hire, be sure to publicly acknowledge their successes and reward them with desirable bonuses. Never forget that without their efforts, your company will not grow.

Here are some ideas for ways to reward sales teams:

- **Choose your own gift.** Set up an account with a corporate gift catalog and let top sellers choose their favorite item within a set budget.

- **Vacation time.** An extra vacation day is an amazingly powerful perk to offer that essentially costs you little.

- **Trips.** If your company gets free-travel offers from resorts looking to drum up business, you could pass one of these along to a top sales-person. Or simply hunt for travel deals to use as awards.

- **Lunch out.** One contest I saw at a news-weekly where I worked had the top salesper-son choosing his or her favorite restaurant and taking several other staffers from other departments out to lunch to celebrate this person's sales win. This served as both a reward and a great company team-develop-ment tool.

- **Money.** Extra cash is always welcomed by hard-working salespeople!

Whatever method you choose for building your sales machine, don't skimp on sales effort. This is the most impor-tant activity at your business, so invest in it accordingly.

Chapter 6

MARKETING

I f sales are the goal of your startup, marketing is the critical activity that helps you reach that goal. Fortunately, there's never been a better time to try to market your business on a shoestring, as the Internet has brought many new free and low-cost ways to get the word out about your business.

If marketing isn't your forte, find a few marketing bloggers to follow, or read books on low-cost marketing. The investment of a few dollars in education will pay off handsomely in less wasted marketing effort. You can also pick up a lot of free tips on social-media forums, such as LinkedIn's Social Media Marketing group.

There are many ways to market your business on the cheap, most of which involve the expenditure of phone time, emails, or shoe leather on your part. I've grouped some of the best approaches below by offline, online, and mobile strategies.

Offline Marketing Strategies

1. **Business cards.** You can get cards free on sites such as VistaPrint. Given that, make up several versions and see what gets the best response. Once you have cards, make sure you always have them with you. You never know when a casual conversation in the supermarket might lead to an opportunity to get a referral. Leave them everywhere—you can even put them in your outgoing bills.

2. **In-person networking.** If you are the main salesperson for your business, get out there and start spreading the word! Attend many different networking events until you find the ones that are good places to connect either directly with your best clients or to people who can refer you to the clients you seek. Though some networking groups such as BNI are costly, there are plenty of free or low-cost networking opportunities.

3. **Join the chamber.** Some local chambers of commerce are quite inexpensive to join. Others can be pricey, so compare and see which local chamber represents the best value for you. A larger chamber located one county over might offer more benefits and better-quality clients than a small-town one. Chamber member benefits often include

listing in a business directory, among other promotional opportunities. If your chamber is expensive, watch for open house events or volunteer with the organization to reduce your dues.

4. **Promotional items.** Cheap promo items can provide long-running marketing benefits, from T-shirts to pencils to magnetic car-door banners. For instance, the caterer who did my son's bar mitzvah had a habit of giving each bar mitzvah boy a hooded sweatshirt with the caterer's company logo on it. Teens love hoodies and tend to live in them. Other kids and their parents then saw the logo repeatedly, reminding them whom to book to cater their own bar mitzvah when the time rolled around. This brand persistence turned our synagogue into a regular account for the caterer, who seemed to cater a bar mitzvah nearly every weekend.

5. **Event sponsorships.** You may think this category is only for deep-pocketed major corporations, but this is just not true. There are sponsorship opportunities at every financial level, and for a business reliant on local customers, they offer great visibility. For instance, my local community does a fundraising drive to put on a Fourth of July fireworks show. I found that for as little as $100, a company

could become a "sponsor" and get recognition in the organizers' newspaper "thank-you" ads for helping make this popular family event possible. What a slam-dunk marketing opportunity for any family-oriented business!

6. **Team sponsorships.** This technique is a century old, and it's still around because it works great for finding local customers. Kids, their families and friends see the shirts with your company name on them repeatedly in the course of a year, long after that charity walk or softball season is over, and they'll often continue wearing them for years to come.

7. **Charity donations.** This is another great local-marketing strategy, particularly for service businesses or retail concepts with high markup. For instance, my husband is a videographer and donated a $500 website video to charity. The donation got him into the charity auction catalog, where everyone in town could read that he's a videographer.

8. **Free product for thought leaders.** This strategy has been employed with success by many companies, including yoga wear retailer lululemon. This is an upscale brand founded in 1998 that charges $98 for a pair of yoga pants, of which you could get a reasonable facsimile for $20 at Target. How do they build

that cachet and make customers crave their better-quality duds?

The company distributes products free to yoga teachers. lululemon's marketing team knows that when the yoga gurus wear lululemon's latest styles, their students will ask about their attire—and then they'll all want to buy one just like it. This approach has helped the company stand out in the very competitive sportswear segment—lululemon cracked $1 billion in sales in 2011.

9. **Toll-free number.** Even though many people now have all-you-can-eat phone calling, a toll-free number will encourage many prospects to give you a call. You can get the number to ring through to your regular phone line—you don't need an extra line. Having a toll-free number communicates to customers that you are expecting national clients and may make your business seem bigger than it might truly be at first. Also, some plans will allow you to pay only for calls made to you or for call minutes used, so this cost will increase only as sales do. Costs range from a nickel to a quarter per minute, the entrepreneur resource Gaebler reports.

10. **Press releases.** You might pay a pro to write a press release and pitch it to the media, or

you could do it yourself. Press releases that contain interesting news can be a low-cost way of getting free publicity for your business in the form of an article in the media. Some internet-based press-release distribution websites, such as PR Log, let you post press releases free. In writing your press release, think about what sort of media your story is best suited for. For instance, if your business offers hot-air balloon rides across a lake, that could make for an interesting, visually oriented TV story, but might be dull for radio. Conversely, if you're opening a kids' gym, that might have some fun audio for a radio story.

11. **Placed articles.** If PR doesn't work, another approach to appearing in print is to write (or have ghostwritten) a how-to, advice, or opinion article with your byline for a local magazine. Business journals and industry trade publications are among the publication types that frequently use these sorts of pieces by local CEOs. Obviously, the more prestigious the publication, the more value you will derive from your placed article. You can expect to pay $500–$1,200 for the article if you hire a professional ghostwriter, but the exposure it can bring your business if printed in the right magazine could bring a great return on investment on that marketing cost.

12. **Public speaking.** Any time you get a chance to speak at an event, you want to do it. Public speaking makes a positive impression on your audience and establishes you as an authority. If you're shy, consider joining Toastmasters to polish up your speaking skills (and do some networking while you're at it).

13. **Grand opening.** If you are opening a physical store, you can get a ton of marketing mileage out of your grand opening. Even a services business might get a mention of its opening in a local business journal. Start by sending out press releases, then follow up on the phone with news media you think would be interested in covering your story. Local newspapers often cover every store opening if they're given enough notice to get out to the event. Offer media more than one angle to cover, such as:

   • Special pre-opening event just for locals
   • [Type of person] opens a store (veteran, single mom, teenager, etc.)
   • New type of store comes to the region (first bagel bakery, bead store, etc.)
   • New store offers discounts on opening week
   • New store offers free items on opening day to first X visitors
   • New store has a contest on opening week

- Serial entrepreneur opens next venture
- Carnival in the parking lot on opening day
- New store brings jobs to the region

14. **Fliers.** If your business is having a sale or special event, putting up fliers on community bulletin boards or under car windshield wipers can create a lot of impressions for your brand for the cost of a little copying and a walk around your town.

Low-Cost Marketing Strategies That Work Well On- and Offline

- **Loyalty cards (both real and virtual).** It's amazing how much people like getting free stuff, such as a free latte or book after they buy ten. Increasingly, physical cards are giving way to online loyalty programs maintained by the business owner, so customers don't have to hang onto a card.

- **Free demonstrations.** If you have a service that's interesting to see in action, see if you could arrange to set up a free demo somewhere you could find a lot of prospects. Trade fairs, such as car or home shows, and local community events are often good locales with a lot of people. Online demonstration videos on your website can also help visitors get more interested in your offering.

- **Free samples.** From sample book-chapter downloads to food tasting at Costco, America loves free samples. This is a proven way to get customers interested and buying at the cost of a small amount of merchandise.

- **Contests.** Almost as much as we love guaranteed free stuff, we love to compete to win free stuff. Online, contests have become a common technique for driving traffic or creating interest in a product or live event. The digital-product site AppSumo is well known for its limited-time contests during which it will give away valuable items such as a MacBook Air.

- **Reviews.** From a review of your novel in *The New York Times* to a write-up of your app by a technology blogger, when critics talk up your product, it can bring a stampede of new customers. Just ask SPANX's founder, Sara Blakely, who scored the ultimate positive review: She mailed a sample of her first footless pantyhose product to Oprah, who chose to feature it on *The Oprah Winfrey Show* as one of her favorite products of the year in 2000. This caused sales to explode and took Blakely from operating out of a back bedroom to renting her first office. The company has since gone on to top $1 billion in valuation.

- **Free reports.** Many bloggers use free reports to get subscribers to sign up to get their email list for their newsletters—this is a proven way to increase sign-ups. Similarly, speakers at conferences will often hand out a free report to whet listeners' appetites for a paid book or course.

- **Testimonials.** Whether it's in a print brochure or a page on your website, customer testimonials describing how great your product or service is are a sure-fire way to help overcome customers' objections and fears and get them to buy. If you have LinkedIn testimonials, copy them over to your website or brochure. Ideally, get small head shots of your customers to include with your testimonials—seeing your happy customers' faces helps prospects relate and see themselves more easily as future customers.

- **Flash sales.** Upscale clothing stores have held these for decades, and short-time sales have become a huge driver for many successful online clothing websites, such as Gilt. The sales' short duration helps drive customer interest and often convinces vendors to allow luxury merchandise to be discounted that might not ordinarily ever go on sale.

- **Coupons.** This technique dates to the late 1800s, and it's still a proven way to get customers in the door. Methods of distributing coupons include circulars such as ValPak, newspaper inserts, newsletters, and simply slipping them into customers' orders or shopping bags. The Internet has brought new twists to coupons, most notably the rise of group-buying coupons as exemplified by Groupon and its many imitators. If you're considering doing a Groupon-type offer, be cautious. Some merchants have ended up losing money on these offers when too many people took advantage or when the coupon users didn't make other full-margin purchases. Three simple ways to keep a handle on your group coupon offer are: limiting the number of people who can participate; making it a deal you only get with another full-price purchase; and excluding existing customers from the offer.

We've already covered the basics of what a powerful sales tool your website can be in the previous chapter. Besides just having a clean site with good SEO, there are many marketing twists you can apply to selling online.

Ten Online Marketing Strategies

1. **Email marketing.** Email is still the killer app when it comes to reaching audiences, building connections, and making sales. Low-cost email marketing services, such as MailChimp, make it easy to design graphical emails and send them to lists of thousands.

2. Article marketing. If you are a service provider or business consultant, article marketing can help potential customers find you online. You can write short how-to or opinion pieces for platforms such as eZine Articles or Answers.com, which are highly trafficked. This can help build your own website's search results. Article marketing can also help you get found by reporters and bloggers and used as an expert source in stories, another great way to promote your business for free.

3. Social-media profiles. Creating a robust profile on LinkedIn, Twitter, and other social-media platforms can be a quick, free way to get found by potential clients, particularly for service-provider businesses. If you include many key words in your profile that prospects might use to search for your business type, you can create an inbound marketing funnel that sends you leads 24/7. For instance, my LinkedIn profile lists that I am a freelance writer, blogger, journalist, and copywriter— and it's brought me several Fortune 500 clients who found me searching LinkedIn for those writing specialties.

4. Social-media marketing. Many books have been written on this booming channel for getting the word out about your business. The trick of marketing on Twitter, LinkedIn, Facebook, and other channels is that being overtly salesy is frowned upon. You have to be a bit more sophisticated in how you interact in these venues to use them as effective marketing platforms. A few quick tips:

- **Find your customers.** Don't just hop on Twitter and spend hours because you've heard it's popular—figure out where your customers hang out in social media, and be there. They might be on Facebook, or on Brides.com if they're getting married, or maybe on Pinterest if they're visual artists.

- **Create a great handle.** When you create the username for a social-media platform, you have a chance to grab attention and tell people what you do. For instance, franchise consultant Joel Libava is @FranchiseKing on Twitter, which is the branding of his company. His photo even shows him wearing a crown. Make it fun, snappy, and informational.

- **Fill out your profile.** As I mentioned, key words are important here—and a link to your business website, so customers can find you and learn more. Upload an image of yourself or your company logo and get rid of the default graphic such as the Twitter "egg." Lots of spammers have those, so show your face.

- **Learn the ropes.** Each social-media platform has its own flavor and etiquette. Watch the action for a bit so you see what's unique—say, how to use hashtags on Twitter to get found more easily.

- **Be helpful.** Remember that the key word in social media is "social." Be conversational and interesting. Most of your posts here should be forwarding useful links to information you found that you think would help your customers in some way. Sales messages should be infrequent and not pushy.

- **Ask for help.** People like to feel useful in social media, so give them opportunities to help you. For instance, one way that I keep reminding people in social media that I'm a freelance writer is by posting on LinkedIn and Twitter about needs I have for sources for upcoming articles. People love to refer me sources, I've found. I'm not selling anything or asking for work in these status updates, but it reminds people I'm a writer.

- **Forget the robots.** Many websites promise to get you thousands of Twitter followers for a few bucks. You can ignore those. The traffic they bring isn't targeted or useful—you won't find customers this way.

- **Follow and engage with thought leaders.** Who are the people who matter to your customers in social media? Find those trendsetters and follow them. Share and respond to their posts, and try to get their attention. Then, try targeting some of your helpful information to them in hopes they will share it with their own audience and help grow yours.

- **Create useful stuff to share.** Whether it's blog posts, a newsletter, a white paper, or other content, most businesses that are successful in social media offer unique, valuable information to their audience.

- **Get organized.** To keep social media from eating all your time, use a scheduler such as HootSuite or Twitter's Tweetdeck. These tools let you create all the messages for the day or even the week or longer; set them to post at various times, and then you're done.

5. **Free webinars and podcasts.** Free live virtual events have become a marketing staple for many consultants and book authors. Platform prices vary greatly, but you can get started with free ones such as Anymeeting.

6. **Blogging.** A company blog can be a great way to create a steady stream of content to share in social media. It can also help customers get to know your business and feel more comfortable buying from you. The biggest problem with starting a blog is that people expect blogs to be regularly updated—so ask yourself if you might outsource this task, or if you have the time to keep up a blog on your own. As with social media, blog posts should not be a series of sales ads. What

should you write about? Here are some proven business-blogging topics that tend to get more comments and social sharing:

- Customer success story
- Contest
- Reader poll or survey
- Contest or poll results
- Your take or disagreement with a popular blogger's post
- Link roundup of useful resources, i.e., 10 Top Italian Chefs for a cooking-supply company
- Your take on a current event in the news that impacts your industry
- Intriguing question about your type of products or your industry
- Your take on industry trends
- Prediction about where your industry is going
- News of what your company plans to do next
- Review of a book, product, or service in your niche
- Video or podcast—store or plant tours are great
- Profile of a staff member or department
- Request for feedback on a new product prototype
- Report on your trip to an industry conference or trade show
- Photo essay spotlighting the charity work of your business

- Your idols—the mentors who inspired you
- Debate that features someone controversial who disagrees with you
- Mistakes you made in the business and what you learned
- Your startup story: What were you doing before? Where did the idea come from?
- Highlight of a good day or great moment in the history of your business
- "A day in the life"—an hour-by-hour journal of what it takes to run your business
- Research the top keywords that bring visitors to your site—then write posts on those topics
- How-to guide
- Tips and tricks—little-known features or creative ways to use your product
- Celebrity Q&A—get a known personality to answer a few questions
- Comparison post that notes advantages of your offerings versus others'

7. **Guest blogging.** Once you're blogging, one of the best ways to grab attention for your blog is through guest posts on popular blogs. Approach bloggers you think your customers read to see if you can guest post. Many big blogs accept guest posts and even post submission guidelines. I personally know quite a few solopreneur business owners who get

most of their clients through their guest posts on prominent blogs. Most guest posts are unpaid, but the hour or two you spend writing them can pay off in high visibility and great client leads.

8. **Google Places for Business and more.** If you have a physical location, you can help customers find you by claiming and enhancing your listing in this Google business directory which is part of the portal's own social-media network, Google+. Other portals where you can claim a business listing include Bing Business Portal and Yahoo! Local.

9. **How-to and "haul" videos.** Adding videos demonstrating your product or service is a proven way to keep customers on your website longer and turn more of them into buyers.

If your product appeals to a young audience, you might find success paying a video blogger to feature it on his or her YouTube channel. Quite a few young women fashionistas have created businesses in which they are paid by retailers to shop their stores and then make a video discussing their finds—the "haul" they brought back from the store. Major retailers, such as Macy's and JCPenney, have used haul bloggers as part of their marketing plan, and you can, too.

Australian startup Shoes of Prey used haul videos to help launch its business in late 2009. The company paid popular video blogger Blair Fowler (known on YouTube as JuicyStar07) to hold a contest in which the winner got a pair of the company's custom-made shoes. The mention on Fowler's popular site gave Shoes of Prey 200,000 site visits in a single day, and 90,000 people entered its contest (the company had hoped for 5,000). While this strategy involves a substantial upfront cost, as this example shows it can pay off in an almost instant mass audience for your product.

10. **Google Analytics.** Whatever types of online marketing you do, the most important thing is to assess the results of each marketing activity so you can adjust your strategy and improve your results. Google Analytics is free and fairly robust in the variety of ways you can slice-and-dice your information on pageviews, sources of traffic, traffic per day, and more.

The most important thing to know about marketing a startup is this: You'll need to experiment. Try different strategies on a small scale, then analyze which marketing activities got the best response and evolve your marketing plan accordingly.

Chapter 7

COLLABORATION AND PARTNERSHIPS

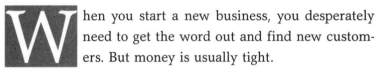hen you start a new business, you desperately need to get the word out and find new customers. But money is usually tight.

One great solution is to find ways to team up with other businesses that need attention, to do events and other marketing activities together. This shares the marketing burden and lowers costs for everyone.

Every type of business can benefit from partnering and collaborative promotion. Here are examples of how both online and retail businesses have used these strategies:

CASE STUDY: DRAWING WOMEN SHOPPERS

When you're just one small women's clothing boutique, it's hard to create excitement about your store. Band together with ten or so other retailers that have women customers, and you can create a Girls Night Out event. Here's the basic structure:

All the participating stores contribute small freebie items to a "goodie bag" shoppers get when they register for the event. Stores also contribute coupons for discounted goods that night. The goodie bag has a low price tag, $10-$15. Often, there is a lower presale price for the goodie bag and a higher one if you buy it on the night of the event.

The price raised by the goodie bags goes to a women's charity—say, Susan G. Komen for the Cure. This charity angle helps shoppers feel they're benefiting a good cause as well as getting bargains.

On the event evening, all the stores have special activities going on—they serve hors d'oeuvres, have a fashion show, offer discounts, or hold sales. Local restaurants are enlisted to offer special deals to Girls Night Out shoppers, too, so they linger in the shopping district longer and spend more.

My local Girls Night Out event from May 2012 reported that the participating merchants took in an extra $18,000 due to this event. Of course, the residual effect in the future of new patrons who discovered stores on that night isn't included in that total.

CASE STUDY: HOW A HIDDEN-AWAY STORE RANG UP BIG SALES

An upscale toy store opened in my Seattle neighborhood, but it didn't have a great location. It was hidden away in the back of a mixed-use complex of doctors' offices and retailers. I wondered how this store was going to survive with little or no walk-in traffic.

Then, one night, I went to a math-game party at my children's public elementary school. The stated purpose was to encourage our children's interest in math. The gym was full of tables of different math games appropriate to all the elementary grades. At least 200 people attended, and everyone had a great time.

At the end of the event, the principal came to the podium to thank the shop that had provided the games: The toy store!

This store couldn't have gotten 200 people in its doors all at once to test out its games on a bet. But through this school collaboration, the shop owners were able to show their core audience—parents of grade-schoolers—the unusual and educational games they stocked, and created terrific buzz among parents about the store.

In the hallway, as families exited, the toy store had a table with their games for sale, which was mobbed with parents, snapping up their kids' favorite math games. They probably sold more in that one night than they had in months. If you have a product that has an educational aspect to it, explore whether your local schools might welcome your help in planning an event. With education budgets being cut everywhere, you might be surprised at their willingness to have you sponsor a school event.

CASE STUDY: TURNING AROUND A SALES SLUMP

When hard times come, a partnership event can bring merchants together and help shoppers become aware of the need to patronize local businesses for the economic health of the community. In my small downtown, the merchants were devastated by a double hit: the down economy of 2009–2011 and a major construction project on the main drag that saw numerous delays and seemed to last forever. Things were looking gloomy.

As construction concluded, the merchants in the neighborhood decided to draw attention to the street's reopening and celebrate their survival. All the shops collaborated to put on a Dinner in White event. These dinners began in France but have since spread over the world as a way to create spontaneous, elegant celebrations and draw people to city centers.

The merchants closed the main street and hosted more than 800 supporters—government officials, best customers, friends and family—for a white-attire, white-tablecloth dinner at long tables set outside, right down the main street. The event drew huge attention—nearly everyone in our city was aware of it, and it was covered extensively by local papers. It sent a big message: Come shop downtown again; the mess is over. It was held on an anniversary of September 11 and also served to commemorate our country's survival of that grim day.

Sitting down with good customers to a gourmet meal on a beautiful evening was a memorable way to build customer relationships. This local event later won a national marketing award as a model for business collaboration in promoting downtown shopping at small stores.

CASE STUDY: AN ONLINE COLLABORATION

When top Internet marketers want to draw attention to their sites and their digital products to create a built-in audience that will be ready to buy a new product, they often enlist the help of dozens of other successful online marketers. This was the case for Danny Iny of Firepole Marketing, a prolific blogger and creator of marketing courses.

Iny wanted to launch a new course and book, *Naked Marketing*, and wrote a manifesto about his marketing concept. But instead of just writing it up himself and trying to promote it alone, he asked more than twenty other prominent bloggers to write a post that would talk about the theme of naked—or honest—marketing and link to the manifesto page.

The campaign resulted in more than 10,000 pageviews and 700 new mailing-list subscribers, Iny says. Off the buzz from this exposure, Iny was able to conduct a successful KickStarter campaign to raise money for the production costs for the print version of the planned book.

Chapter 8

ADVERTISING

Many new entrepreneurs ignore the world of advertising—isn't it so yesterday? A throwback to the '60s world of *Mad Men*? Actually, it isn't, and the form and pay structure for ads is changing fast.

Advertising can get the name of a new business in front of a big audience in a short time. There are many bargains to be had in advertising, too, both online and offline.

Here's a look at the three big legs of today's advertising stool—print, online, and mobile device:

PRINT AD TIPS

You make think print ads are old-school, but the print market is changing, not dying—nearly 313 million copies of print magazines were sold in 2011, the Magazine Publishers of America reported, and more than 200 new magazines launched that year, according to the Association of Magazine Media.

The good news for you as a startup owner is that many print publications are struggling with the poor economy and changes to the publishing industry—which means their ad staff are ready to make a deal. A few tips for getting the best print ad for the least money:

- **Haggle.** Know that, especially in a downturn, the published rate sheet is not necessarily the last word in pricing.

- **Call the day before the deadline.** At this point in the publication cycle, ad sales staffers are desperate to book any additional revenue. You might secure a lingering blank spot in the paper at a fraction of the usual price.

- **Make a package deal.** Ask for a free first ad as a test, on the proviso that if it performs well, you will follow up with a contract for several paid ads.

- **Prorate.** Ask for the rate offered for a twelve-times-a-year commitment for fewer ads, perhaps three or four.

- **Pay for performance.** Online isn't the only place where you can pay for ads based on results. If your print ad links to a unique URL on your website, you can track how much traffic and sales it brought you and pay accordingly. Print publications are increasingly amenable to this type of arrangement, as long as you're willing to share your traffic data.

- **Get perks.** If the ad staff won't budge on price at a large media company, see if you can get an extra ad in a second publication or on a bus bench or billboard thrown into the deal.

- **Do a regional buy.** Many national magazines now offer the ability to purchase a lower-cost ad that will only appear in a particular city or region's print run. This can be a great way to associate yourself with a prominent national magazine at budget prices.

- **Try an ad broker.** Ad brokers buy ad space in bulk on the cheap and then resell it. Connecting with ad brokers may allow you to find deals you wouldn't see otherwise.

- **Hit the movies.** Local-access cable TV shows and movie-theater prescreening ads are two often overlooked areas where ads can get you great local exposure at an affordable price.

- **Broadcast your message.** Local radio, particularly sponsorships on nonprofit radio stations, is often an affordable ad buy.

ONLINE AD TIPS

Online ads have opened up a new world of low-cost advertising. The thrill of online advertising is that, in many instances, there are no minimum budgets or set amounts you must pay. You can design and test campaigns, set small maximum payment amounts, and quickly see what gets results.

Here are tips on ways to spread the word about your brand with Internet-based advertising:

- **Begin with a Craigslist ad.** If you want to test whether a product or service will find a ready audience online, a free Craigslist ad can give you some immediate feedback.

- **Improve your natural search results.** This is probably the best ad deal online—a few hours with a skilled SEO specialist who gets your site to the top of your desired key-word searches saves your having to buy ads on portals such as Google. And consumers increasingly favor natural search results over paid ads placed on top of or alongside natural search results.

- **Consider pay-per-impression.** Banners or text ads may charge on the basis of how many viewers are exposed to the ad. Per-impression rates are usually the lowest of any online-ad formula, but beware—impressions do not equal sales or even leads you can follow up. These types of campaigns are best when you're simply looking to build brand aware-ness rather than immediately converting viewers to buyers.

- **Consider pay-per-click (PPC).** This is a common form of online ad. Rates are a bit higher, but you only pay if viewers engage with your ad. If you have a successful strategy for capturing these prospects' emails from the ad so you can market to those leads in the future, PPC can be a good way to go.

- **Consider pay-per-lead.** Many entrepreneurs prefer pay-per-lead, a refinement of PPC, as often clicks don't mean much—the customer might have clicked by accident or might leave your site after a single second. Pay-per-lead discards these quick-bounce visits, so you only pay for prospects who appear to be seriously checking out your offer.

- **Consider pay-per-sale.** Some advertising platforms also offer this option. Rates are the highest of these three methods, but you have the advantage of being able to pay the ad bill out of actual sales.

- **Target unsold space.** Another approach is to look for websites that have a sidebar full of small ads. If there is a "your ad here" or filler ad in place, you know there is an unsold spot where you might be able to negotiate a discount rate.

- **Use ad networks.** Sophisticated ad networks can help you find a smaller and hence more affordable demographic slice by appearing only in search results for certain types of Internet visitors, such as women aged eighteen to twenty-one who have recently bought shoes.

- **Be a resource.** Many professional organizations offer a resource page on their website for their members that showcases service providers to their industry. If you offer a service such as accounting, legal, writing, or web design, contact organizations for your target customers and inquire if they allow resource listings. There may be a small charge, or the listing might be free, depending on the group. My experience is that many organizations will list you as a resource free— and they rarely review or update these pages, so your listing could persist for years.

Case Study: Facebook Ads

E-commerce pet-food seller PetFlow used Facebook ads extensively in building its massive Facebook audience, says cofounder Alex Zhardanovsky. His tip: Advertise simply to attract the right demographic to your page rather than to sell a particular product.

PetFlow places simple Facebook ads targeted only to pet owners to narrow the size of the audience and reduce ad cost. Simple messages such as "Do you like cats? Click here . . ." or "Got a cute cat picture? Add yours here" helped get the right people onto the Facebook page.

From there, customers see occasional short-time and closeout sale deals PetFlow posts only to Facebook, turning those Facebook "likes" into paying customers. Using this strategy, the startup was able to grow its fan base to more than 512,000. In mid-June 2012, PetFlow was recognized as the top retail or e-commerce brand for Facebook fan engagement—passing major brands, including Walmart, Target, Converse, and Nike.

MOBILE AD METHODS

The use of smartphones is growing—more than two-thirds of the world's population had a mobile-phone subscription in 2011, and 87 percent of Americans had a smartphone. The devices have become an increasingly viable channel for low-cost marketing campaigns. Mobile-ad strategies include:

- **Text messaging (SMS).** Get customers to opt in to your text-messaging list, and you can send them quick updates about new products or sale items. Text-messaging providers such as EzTexting and Moto Message help you create the codes and keywords needed to reach out to customers this way. Many platforms have a free trial so you can check them out, and paid levels start at $17 a month. For instance, one regional Seattle-area movie-theater operator created its own loyalty card system through email marketing and SMS text messages. Using a card printer already on the premises, the chain sold $20 reward cards and captured buyers' smartphone numbers in the process. On slow nights, the theaters can sell more seats by texting cardholders to offer them a discount on that night's shows.

- **Multimedia messaging (MMS).** Take your mobile message to a more sophisticated level by including pictures, sound, and additional text.

- **Mobile email.** Email marketing hits the smartphone with new methods of capturing emails, such as running campaigns that ask customers to text you their email address.

- **Mobile search.** Services such as FourSquare are making it easier for traveling customers to find a nearby service or product they need. Including maps and directions that are viewable on mobile devices (most Flash-built site elements aren't easily viewable) can bring you more customers who are searching on the fly.

- **QR codes.** The hot new kid on the marketing block, Quick Response barcodes can quickly send smartphone users to more information about your business on your website. Free QR-code makers are proliferating and make it easy for your business to jump on this trend.

- **Mobile apps.** If you can turn your service into a mobile application, or develop one that enables customers to play games or otherwise interact with your products, you can jump on this hot trend and do anything from building brand awareness to capturing more sales. Appmakr and dozens of other free services can help you create an app for your business.

- **Mobile advertising.** The growth of online magazines with mobile-app versions means that a specialty market for mobile ads is growing, too.

Mobile advertising also offers new opportunities to engage customers. For instance, smartphones come with cameras, allowing for promotions in which customers email photos of themselves using your product to your Facebook page to get a discount coupon. Experiment with the possibilities for your business—mobile ads are an emerging arena for low-cost marketing techniques.

One recent promotion McDonald's did in Europe shows the potential for mobile engagement with customers. The chain set up giant electronic billboards in a busy city square that enabled smartphone users passing by to play games on the billboards, using their smartphones as game controllers. Winners got small, free food items redeemable at the nearest McDonald's store, which got diners choosing the Golden Arches' fast-food restaurants over nearby competitors' eateries.

Chapter 9

FACILITIES

S ome businesses can go on indefinitely operating out of a spare room in your house or can be run from your laptop while you lounge at the local coffeehouse. If this is you, you can skip this chapter.

Many types of business, though, need an office or store at which to meet customers, or a warehouse for storing product prior to shipment or delivery. If you need a physical place for your business, move very cautiously as you select your space.

Renting, buying, or leasing a facility will add a substantial fixed monthly cost to your business, so make sure you don't overspend. Often, new business owners plunge ahead and sign a one-year lease right away, obligating the owner for twelve preset, monthly lease payments that will be due no matter how poorly the business does.

Too often, once that facilities decision is made, the business is headed for an unhappy ending. Within a few months, the owner realizes one or more of the following:

- This isn't the best location for this business

- The space is bigger than needed, so the rent is too much

- The lease rate is too high relative to what the business will earn

- This business idea isn't going to work without changes

- Those changes to the business model require a different type of facility

From there, it's a death march to the end of the lease. The owner might long to close the business and move on to their next business idea—or to move the business to a more appropriate site—but is trapped by the lease contract.

Now the owner continues to operate the business mainly because he's desperately trying to cover the lease obligation so he doesn't sink into debt. Often, businesses in this boat close up and vanish the minute the lease is up, yet another victim of too much overhead.

Don't let this happen to you. Begin with the philosophy that you want to delay making any facilities commitment for as long as possible. Once you make the well-considered decision that you need a facility, strive to keep your footprint—and your lease obligation—as small as possible. This chapter spotlights an array of strategies for reducing or eliminating your facilities costs.

COULD YOU START VIRTUAL?

The first question to ask is whether you could postpone a facilities commitment until after you've launched and been in business for a few months. Increasingly, smart entrepreneurs are road-testing their concepts with online stores or by operating out of their homes before deciding to pay rent on a business space. A dose of real-world experience in your business may change your ideas about the type of facility you need.

You might be surprised how easily you can project the image that you have a professional, successful business without a swanky office or sleek retail shop. I once met the founder of an Internet-security research firm that targeted major government agencies. I assumed he would need a plush office in the thick of the action in Washington, D.C., for meetings with high-powered clients.

But he related that he started the business as a virtual organization, with all of the partners working out of their home offices in various cities. The agency heads he dealt with had no problem with this, and the firm conducted business at the clients' offices, met on virtual platforms online, and signed contracts online and via fax. After getting established, the team concluded that they didn't need to leave their respective homes, and continued to operate virtually as the organization grew.

The lesson here? *Challenge the assumption that you need a facility.*

If you're a retailer, consider starting as an e-commerce-only operation to test the market and see if there is consumer interest. If you get some response, then you can explore whether a physical locale would drive more business. If so, then it's time to research where that facility should be located and whether that sales increase would be enough for the facility costs to pencil out.

Product manufacturers or inventors can look to get their product placed on an existing retailer's shelves. This is a far more cost-efficient way to get your product in front of consumers—piggybacking on the known quantity of an established chain—compared with opening and trying to staff and promote your own store.

If you've decided you need a physical space, your goal should be to keep it as small as possible. Here are ten options to consider when starting with a small facilities commitment:

1. **Kiosk or cart.** One of the notable retail success stories in Seattle is that of jewelry retailer Something Silver. This Northwest chain today has nine locations, including two high-traffic stores at Disneyland theme parks. But Something Silver didn't launch by opening a store.

    Cofounders Cheri and Tony Swan started the business in 1994 with a single small cart that sat in the aisle at the Northgate Mall, a popular shopping center north of Seattle.

Despite the fact that most malls already had more than one jewelry store, the Swans felt there was room for a new concept in jewelry—a lower-priced store that primarily featured silver jewelry, not pricey wedding rings on gold bands.

In its first year of operation, Something Silver proved its concept. Annual sales from this tiny mall kiosk soon reached $360,000. Mall owner Simon Property Group—the nation's top mall operator—informed the Swans that their cart had the most sales of all cart operators at *all* of its malls! This gave the pair the confidence to expand to a retail store, and their proven sales track record also helped the Swans secure a $100,000 SBA-backed bank loan to cover store-opening costs.

Contrast this success story with what happened to a couple of women entrepreneurs in a neighborhood near Seattle who wanted to sell their homemade ice cream. They created some interesting ice cream flavors and leased a large, open-air shop space near a local movie theater for $2,000 a month.

Once they opened, the women made some unhappy discoveries. Traffic inside the mall where the theater was located wasn't nearly what they'd hoped. Also, the cinema didn't allow outside food into the theaters.

Additionally, the mall rules required them to be open long hours. The stress of losing money while operating with this high overhead broke up the partnership, and as soon as the one-year lease was up, the business closed.

One partner rethought the business model and went in a new direction: She purchased a refrigerated ice cream cart. She began taking the cart to community events, everything from Fourth of July parades to public-school carnivals. There were huge crowds at each event, and she sold ice cream cones as fast as she could scoop them up for the brief span of each event.

She later confessed to me that this model was highly profitable and afforded her a better lifestyle, too. She made more working a day or two a week than she had in that fixed-location ice cream shop working six days a week! With her cart, she didn't spend long hours waiting for customers and had plenty of time left for family.

As you can see, a cart or kiosk can offer many advantages, including lower overhead costs and mobility to get your product in front of your audience, wherever they might be.

2. **Food or retail truck**. If you're thinking about opening a retail store or restaurant, a lower-risk

way to try out your concept is to put it on wheels. A food or merchandise truck can easily test out different neighborhood locations to find the best one. As you travel around, you can also build interest in your brand, giving you a built-in audience if you eventually settle on a fixed location.

Here are the stories of two entrepreneurs who built their businesses by going mobile:

CASE STUDY: SKILLET STREET FOOD

Starting with a truck proved the success route for Seattle restaurant Skillet Diner. The business began in 2007 with a single food truck, Skillet Street Food, which cost about $20,000 to put on the road, recalls cofounder Josh Henderson. At the time, there were few food trucks circulating in downtown Seattle.

Henderson says the eatery's approach—presenting high-quality food rather than the usual taco-truck fare—was an instant hit with Seattleites, who monitored Skillet's Facebook and Twitter pages for news of where the truck was parked. In 2010, Skillet added a second truck to keep up with demand, paying $50,000 to have it better equipped for the rigors of cooking on the road.

The food trucks served as mobile advertisements for Skillet's food, which also won raves from local restaurant critics. But the trucks also have their limitations—tiny kitchens that can only crank out so much food at a time, and a seasonal business in which diners disappear if it rains.

By the time Henderson sought a permanent restaurant space for Skillet Diner and needed to raise money for the more than $500,000 opening cost, Skillet was a well-known and highly regarded name among Seattle foodies. Given the brand's high profile in town, it wasn't hard to find an investor to help with the restaurant opening costs.

The opening of Skillet Diner in Seattle's Capitol Hill neighborhood in 2011 was an instant hit thanks to the awareness built by the trucks.

"It all paid forward when we opened the diner," Henderson says. "It became exceptionally successful and enabled us to grow our business."

CASE STUDY: BIKER BABES AND BEYOND

One entrepreneur who has seen success with a retail truck is Julia Hutton. She initially opened a traditional store that sold motorcycle accessories for women, Biker Babes and Beyond, in Prescott, Arizona. The business was successful and opened a second location.

Then came the downturn of 2008, and business slumped. A former marketing executive, Hutton thought creatively and decided to take her merchandise on the road, to motorcycle rallies.

She soon discovered she could sell more goods at a weekend bike rally than she sold at one of her Biker Babes retail stores in a week. The mobile store concept was so successful that Hutton started another business, Extreme ReTrailers, which leases custom 7' x 14' trucks outfitted with retail fixtures to other entrepreneurs.

3. **Trunk show**. Rather than paying big rent for a permanent home, many great businesses have been launched on the home-party or "trunk show" model. Well-known names from Tupperware to Mary Kay make sales at home parties. Trunk shows are also a great sales method for startup entrepreneurs—especially if they band together.

   A local example from my own neighborhood is Indie Banditas Traveling Bazaar, a collective of roughly thirty handmade-goods crafters who put on one-day sales events at various local venues. One recent Indie Banditas event was held in the common room of a local nursing home.

   You can imagine how cheap it is to rent the hall of a nursing home for a single day compared with leasing a store year-round—which, for a time, Indie Banditas did. Now, the artists' collective is living happily ever after, with no permanent rent to pay and a short-sale model that creates excitement about products—and then leaves all the artists with plenty of time to go home and do more crafting rather than having to take turns staffing a retail store counter.

4. **Coworking office**. If you need a professional office—either because your home doesn't have space for an office or because you need

an office for client meetings—consider a coworking facility before getting a stand-alone office of your own. A coworking office is usually a large, open-plan office space where solopreneurs and telecommuters work independently on their own business endeavors. Many amenities may be included, such as high-speed Internet connections, computer terminals, faxing and copy privileges, and closed-door conference rooms for private meetings or phone calls.

One of the key advantages here is flexibility—instead of paying for rent every minute of every day of the month, even days when you're closed, you pay only for the amount of office time you need. You might secure a permanent desk, where you set up in the same place each day, or have a floating desk and pay less. Most coworking offices have flexible rental plans that allow you to come in every day during regular hours, get an after-hours pass for unlimited use, or contract to use the space just a few days a week. You might either bring your laptop and other office supplies or store them on site in a locker.

Presto! You have a professional-looking office that appears to be bustling with activity when clients arrive to meet with you.

Besides the potential cost-savings, coworking offers other advantages. Often, coworking sites offer many networking opportunities, so you might find clients among your fellow coworkers or receive referrals from them.

Coworking is booming—a survey by the online workspace magazine *DeskMag* reported in 2011 that the number of coworking desks available worldwide had doubled annually since 2006 to top 1,100 desks. Check with your chamber or do a little Internet research to see if there is a coworking space near you. Two growing chains of coworking facilities are The Hub, which has more than 25 locations worldwide, and NextSpace, which has five California locations.

5. **Temporary store**. During the holiday season, a funny thing happens at many shopping malls: All the empty stores in the mall suddenly fill up. The mall is chock-full for Christmas! Then, in January, many of the stores empty out again.

What happened here? The malls rented to some merchants on a short-term basis during the peak season. This is a win-win situation: The landlords want their malls to feel busy and full for shoppers, and the short-term merchants get a high-visibility store space during the prime selling time without having to make a lengthy lease commitment. Short-term lease deals are often a bargain, as you're really meeting a need the landlord has, while also fulfilling your own desire to sell goods in the mall.

If you have merchandise that is sold mostly during a specific time of year, a temporary store can cut your overhead while still letting you grab shoppers' attention and ring up most of the sales you'd capture if you operated your store year-round. In recent years, even big national chains have caught on to the advantages of short-term or "pop-up" stores. This model is such a great one that there are successful businesses built entirely around the idea of operating only seasonally, such as Halloween Express, which operates year-round online but opens stores only around October.

A temporary store gives you a chance to experiment with your store's look and feel, as well as with your product mix, without having to make a long-term facility commitment. For instance, in 2011 handbag brand Kate Spade opened an arresting-looking igloo-shaped pop-up store in a New York City park to sell holiday goods, and Japanese accessories trendsetter Uniqlo erected tiny cube-shaped stores in downtown Manhattan. Pop Tarts and The Gap are among the other big brands that have used pop-ups to grab attention. The temporary nature of the store may also help drive sales as shoppers know they should buy now because the store will soon be gone.

Another common example of a seasonal-store setup is on view at your local farmer's market. Stall vendors are open one or two days a week, spring to fall. That leaves plenty of other time free to work on your business, as you're not standing behind a counter forty hours a week.

When Brad Gruno was starting Brad's Raw Chips, he first tested his chips on shoppers at four different Pennsylvania farmer's markets. The feedback he got there helped him build the company into a more than $2 million business in two years. Brad's is now found in Whole Foods Markets and many other major grocery stores.

6. **Trade show booth**. If you have a new product or service, rather than opening an office or store, consider debuting it at a trade show. Often, small booths can be rented at a fairly affordable rate—or you could just attend and talk up your product at networking events at the conference. Trade shows bring together a concentrated audience of one type of buyer—say, homeowners at a home show—which gives you a great opportunity to get exposure to many possible buyers in a short time.

To pick up Brad Gruno's story, once he had worked a few farmer's markets, his next stop was a New York City eco-themed trade show. He saved money by renting part of a booth from another vendor who sold raw salsa. Brad's raw chips were a natural complement to the other vendor's product, drawing more interest than either entrepreneur likely would have seen renting a solo booth. Gruno recalls, however, that the chips were the hit of the booth—soon they were all gone!

"Within two hours, I had a crowd of people around me, and they didn't care about the salsa," he says. "I went, 'Wow—I think there might be a need for this.'"

For some vendors, trade shows are the only "store" needed—they meet all their customers on the trade-show floor and make their sales, then go home to create more products.

7. **Sublet.** Here is a tale of two food-service businesses, one of which thrived whereas the other failed and had to be sold:

The first business was started by a young mother who wanted to open a gluten-free cake bakery. Instead of opening a shop or building an expensive commercial kitchen, she contracted to bake her cakes in the off-hours at a local restaurant, late at night after closing time. The business was a great success using this model. To this day, she hasn't opened a physical store, and she delivers her cakes to customers all over town. She's able to keep the price of her cakes affordable because her overhead is quite low.

The other businesswoman wanted to open a cookie store to make money to help put her son through college. She rented a store and built her own commercial kitchen. This, as you can imagine, involved a substantial up-front cost. The only affordable space she could find for her store was in a less-than-ideal location for a cookie shop—in a business park outside of the main town center.

Unsurprisingly, business was slow. Her cookies were great, but she had a hard time finding steady clients with her out-of-the-way locale. To cover the cost of her build-out, she had to charge steep prices for her cookies, which were delicious, but customers balked at the cost. This business model of high overhead requiring a high product price wasn't successful, and she sold the business and moved away. The new owner promptly moved the store to a smaller space in the center of town, where it reduces overhead by sharing space with a crepes shop.

The moral of our story: *Find excess capacity instead of creating a new facility.* If you need a facility for manufacturing, baking, or producing anything, somewhere in your town there is probably someone who already has that kind of facility. See if you can sublease from him. This is a facilities strategy that can save a fortune, and save your business, too.

Subletting is also a great strategy if you need warehouse space. Network in your community to find warehouse operators who have unused space. Then, cut a deal to use a portion of their square footage. If necessary, create a lockdown space you wall off from their main facility to secure your goods. When distributors or manufacturers have excess warehouse space, it usually means that business is bad (or they would be stocking more product). In this situation, they will be only too happy to turn their unneeded space into a little extra income.

8. **Furnish cheap**. Once you've decided to open a facility, the next challenge is to equip and furnish that facility. You may need office furniture or retail racks. But whatever you need, there's a low-cost way to buy it: shop liquidation sales.

Every day, businesses go bust. When they do, the contents of their facilities are often bought up by a liquidation company. One of the biggest retail-store liquidators is Gordon

Brothers Group, which in recent years liquidated the fixtures from all the Borders bookstores. Many more liquidators operate online.

Buying liquidated store or office fixtures can get you the equipment you need at pennies on the dollar of what you would have paid at retail. The range of liquidated items you can get is truly boggling—everything from restaurant equipment to computers and desks to retail store gondolas. Often, goods are in great condition or can be easily spruced up.

9. **Think small**. Some of the most successful retail chains and professional offices have a secret to their success: They operate in a tiny space. Think of how Mrs. Fields revolutionized the dessert-store business by opening tiny mall slots that were hardly wider than a man is tall. Many of the chain's stores retained that small footprint, enabling the franchisees to operate with a very low lease cost.

When Something Silver's owners decided to expand to a full retail store in the mall where they had their cart, the space they used was just 650 square feet. Today, many of their locations are still very small stores. Smaller stores mean lower rent and less sales you have to bring in to break even.

Of course, if you can start from home, there's no immediate facilities cost at all.

When Brad Gruno started Brad's Raw Chips, he first manufactured the product in his own garage. It wasn't until he had signed up health-food stores and the business was on its feet and growing that he moved on to a full-blown manufacturing plant.

10. **Look before you lease: avoiding facilities mistakes**. Many new business owners fall in love with the idea of having a store or an office. It makes them feel legitimate—like they're really in business now! But the decision to open a facility shouldn't be an emotional one. Instead, you want to make sure this facility makes economic sense for your business. Will it enable you to store more product and therefore get volume-buying discounts, for instance? Will a retail store give your business the needed visibility and community awareness?

Another common facilities pitfall is to fall in love with the first store or office or warehouse you see. Maybe they have a special offer going, or a realtor gives you a big pitch because she's hot to make a sale.

Don't get pressured into signing up for a facilities commitment. Just as you should do extensive market research and business planning before you launch your business, do thorough facilities research. Information to gather about prospective facilities could include:

- Traffic counts (How many cars drive by?)
- Foot traffic (How many customers walk by?)
- Tenant history (Have a string of previous tenants gone bust here?)
- Tenant mix (Who else is in the building, and how are they doing?)
- Vacancy rate
- Freeway access
- Parking slots available
- Hours of operation required
- Current condition of unit
- Age of facility
- Potential for expansion on-site
- Landlord assistance available for building out the site
- Lease or purchase terms offered

Know all the possible options for where you could locate your business in your market, and compare the advantages and drawbacks of each before making a final decision.

If you're having trouble deciding on the best choice, do a "pro and con" worksheet of all the reasons to open at your chosen locale— and all the reasons to pass on it. Benchmark the amenities of various facilities against each other in a written list. Seeing all the issues in print should help you make a sound decision that makes sense for your business and your budget.

RENT VERSUS LEASE VERSUS OWN

One of the most important facilities decisions is whether you will buy, lease, or rent. For most entrepreneurs, buying a facility early on is a high-risk gamble: You don't know enough about your business yet to know if this facility will truly serve the long-term needs of your business. You also take on real estate market risk, because if the market declines or goes into a sales slump, you might not be able to sell or sublease. On the plus side, you control the property and can alter it to suit your business without a landlord's interference.

What's the difference between leasing and renting? A lease is usually a long-term agreement of a set, predetermined length, in which you commit to occupy a facility for a period of years or at least one year. Often, there will also be options to renew for additional years, with increases prenegotiated and defined up front. Many prime retail locations, such as top-performing malls, will require a long-term lease to sign you up as a tenant.

By contrast, a rental may have more of a month-to-month agreement. Renting can be ideal for startups as the commitment to continue renting is low. But there's a flip side—it also means the landlord is free to toss you out if he finds a better tenant. Also, month-to-month agreements mean the landlord is free to raise your rent at any time, which brings some uncertainty to your overhead costs.

Seven Tips for Negotiating Your Facility Deal

1. **Research, research, research.** Find out what rents are going for in your market for this type of space, and know what amenities are usually offered.

2. **Ask for a tenant improvement budget.** Especially if times are tough and the landlord has a lot of vacancies, you might be surprised at how much money the landlord could be willing to invest to recarpet, repaint, or otherwise upgrade your facility to get you to move in.

3. **Request a free period.** Ask the landlord if you can have the first three months free if you sign a longer-term lease commitment. This could buy you valuable breathing space to get your business going.

4. **Arrange for revenue-based rent.** Some landlords are willing to set a low base rent and then take a cut of actual revenue. This can be a good situation for a startup as your initial rent will be lower, and then you'll pay more only when you make more.

5. **Aim for a short term.** Try for six months on an initial lease instead of a year commitment, or a year but then month-to-month from there on. This gives you a quicker out if the location proves a mistake.

6. **Get utilities included.** This can be a real money-saver if your type of business uses a lot of electricity or gas.

7. **Ask for delayed payments.** If the landlord is hard up for tenants, he might be willing to have you pay the first six months' rent all at the end of month six.

Once you decide on the right facilities footprint for your budding business, remember that everything is negotiable. Get the best facilities deal you can to keep your fixed costs low.

Chapter 10

OPERATIONS

O nce your business gets going, you'll begin spending money, often at a terrifying pace. Day-to-day operations costs can be a squishy area that doesn't receive enough cost-cutting scrutiny, as what you're doing all seems essential to making the business run.

Just remember that every cost of getting your business done cuts into your profits, so keep your focus on frugality when you look at your operating costs.

Operating costs come in two types: Fixed costs and variable costs. An example of a fixed cost is the monthly Internet bill. A variable cost might be the cost of repairing equipment when it breaks down.

While it's harder to predict and control variable or one-time costs, both cost types should receive scrutiny for possible cost cutting. Both types have particular challenges, too. Fixed recurring costs are easy to forget about or accept as an unavoidable cost of doing business—don't let that happen. Furthermore, variable costs often pop up unexpectedly, and it's easy to end up overspending under the pressure to keep operations going and solve problems quickly.

Any recurring fixed cost you have should be reevaluated and put out for new, independent bids on at least an annual basis if not more frequently. New service providers come on the market, and existing providers come up with new discount offers—make sure you know about them so you can take advantage.

One-time costs should also be competitively bid whenever possible. Also evaluate whether dealing with the "emergency" could actually be delayed to a future point.

We will cover a few key aspects of operational cost in the following chapters on purchasing, logistics, and labor. Those areas aside, here is a rundown on all the aspects of operations where you may find opportunities to save money:

RAW MATERIALS

If you are a manufacturer, you purchase supplies or components with which to make your product. If you operate a restaurant, you need the raw ingredients with which you will make your dishes.

The cost of these raw materials should be aggressively monitored by comparing multiple vendors on a regular basis. Also explore whether substitute materials might be available that could deliver a similar-quality product with a lower cost.

SERVICES

Many businesses require the services of independent professionals and service-providing companies. This list may include:

- Attorney

- Accountant

- Exterminator

- Trash hauler

- Cleaning service

- Web designer or developer

- High-speed Internet provider

- Mailing list management service

- E-commerce shopping cart provider

- Computer-backup service

- Landline and/or cell phone service

The first question to ask yourself about each of these services is: Could you do it yourself?

For instance, I've paid for curbside trash pickup for my home-based freelance writing business, but when I lost a big client and needed to tighten my belt, my family started packing our trash into the car and hauling it to the dump ourselves to save about $50 a month.

Could you clean your own office? Do your own taxes? Not scared of filling out legal forms on your own? If you can and have the time to do such tasks yourself, they become money-saving opportunities.

If you can't do these tasks, shop for the best deal. Maybe you could trade goods or services with one of these needed professionals and avoid some of the out-of-pocket costs. If not, get competitive bids and ask for discounts for signing a one-year contract. I've seen freelancers build their own email-marketing databases in Excel to keep from paying for a customer-relationship management service, for instance.

Services such as utilities—which used to have fixed costs and you were stuck with a single provider—are now wide-open to competition. A great example is phone service. Long-distance calling was once prohibitively expensive, but now you can call internationally for free or cheap using tools such as Voice Over Internet Portocol (VOIP)-based Skype or Keku, which assigns you a local number in the country where you wish to call.

SUPPLIES

This category covers everything you need to purchase for your business that doesn't end up getting sold to your customer. If you have an office, you might need office supplies such as pencils, pens, copy paper, writing pads, and fax-machine toner. If you operate a retail store, you might need bags, toilet paper, and paper towels.

Often, businesses sign up with one supplier for office needs and then basically forget about it. Every time you need supplies, you pull out that same catalog and place an order.

This is not a good approach, as all suppliers will have items they make more margin on and lower-profit ones.

Instead, compare several suppliers and cherry-pick items between them. Keep accounts with more than one supplier so it's easy to order from a competitor to get a better deal. Also, feel free to play suppliers off against each other to see if one might offer to beat the other's price.

If you have employees, be careful about who has the power to approve and order supplies. Make sure workers don't treat your supply catalog as a candy store to order whatever goodies they feel the office should stock.

For instance, a movie production office where I once worked would send a worker to Costco once a month with a blank check to buy snacks for the office kitchen. You never saw so many snacks in an office in your life! Instead, have a supplies budget, stick to it, and closely oversee purchases. Have a supply request sign-up form—then review it and only approve what is truly needed.

SOFTWARE AND THE CLOUD

These days, small businesses of all types are increasingly reliant on technology to run their operations. These tools may be physical software programs you purchase at a store, download onto your computer, or lease from remote servers offered by a software-as-a-service company. You may have programs that track your product shipping, cloud-based data-storage providers, and much more.

In every case, consider whether there is a free version of any software or cloud-based services you use, or a lower-cost provider. See the e-commerce chapter for more details on free options here.

For instance, in my consulting and teaching business I use webinar platforms to present to students all over the world. I have tried and discarded several webinar service providers over the course of a few years as I discovered lower-cost providers with easier-to-use platforms. I began with a platform for which I paid $100 and could only host 100 people at a time. Over time, I progressed to one where I can host 500 people for just $67 a month.

There is hardly an application or software-based service that does not have reams of competition, so be sure to explore your options. Many online-service businesses also offer free-trial versions of their services for thirty days or longer. If you're clever and willing to learn new systems, you might go for months on the free trials of several different providers.

ENERGY COSTS

Depending on your business type, you may use a variety of traditional energy sources—electricity, natural gas, coal, or propane, for example. Good news for you: deregulation has brought competition to many markets. If you have more than one option for a utility provider, be sure to compare to see if one would cost less.

David Mattocks, a green-energy consultant with the international firm Green Pro Systems, says, "Most business owners way underestimate the amount they can save on their energy bill. You think of it as a fixed cost, but it's not. You can cut it in half."

Beyond your choice of provider, one of the easiest ways to save money in business is to reduce your energy use, especially if you have a physical facility. There is almost always energy waste that could be cut.

Low-Cost Energy Saving Ideas

- **Switch bulbs.** It's an up-front cost, but if you switch from incandescent to more energy efficient LED or compact fluorescent lamps, you can dramatically reduce your electricity bills over time. Compact fluorescents also have a much longer lifespan, so you will be paying for replacements less often.

- **Add timers on lights.** Take a hint from every convenience-store bathroom you've ever visited, and put a timer on lights in little-used rooms. That will keep lights from accidentally being left on.

- **Install motion-enabled switches.** These timers go one step better, flicking lights on automatically when someone enters a room and turning them off again when a sensor detects they have left.

- **Turn down thermostats.** At our house, we wear sweaters and turn the thermostat down to 59 degrees. You should also close off the vents in any unused rooms.

- **Turn devices all the way off.** Computers, TVs and other modern devices draw some power, even when they're off. Unplug items from the wall to prevent them from drawing power in their "off" hours.

- **Insulate.** If you own your place of business, consider getting an energy audit from your local utility company. It's usually free, and the utility will help you identify cost-effective ways to add insulation around doors, in attics, and other heat-loss areas to cut your utility bills.

- **Switch energy types.** If you are using an expensive form of energy, research whether you might switch. For instance, where I live, electricity is expensive and natural gas is unavailable, so many restaurants buy a tank and cook with cheaper propane gas.

CASE STUDY: TREEHOUSE CAFÉ

If you are looking to reduce your energy costs, know that there are government and nonprofit programs that may help you with the up-front costs of your reduction program. One busy Puget Sound–area restaurant, Treehouse Café, partnered with the nonprofit Foundation for Responsible Technology in Carson City, Nevada, to run a campaign in which cafe customers contributed a small surcharge—1 percent of their cafe meal costs—with each purchase going toward the $3,000 that the cafe needed to install energy-efficient lightbulbs.

The nonprofit provided software that added the donation appeal to the bottom of each credit card statement.

Seattle is a region with a highly ecologically aware citizenry. Customers were surprisingly receptive to the idea of helping the restaurant save energy. Within six months, Treehouse owner Arnie Sturham says, the eatery raised the needed funds to install the new bulbs. The projected savings are $1,800 a year, so within two years, the initiative would deliver bottom-line savings to the restaurant.

HOURS OF OPERATION

If you have office or store hours, one easy way to cut down labor, janitorial, supply, and utility costs is to reduce your hours. Many retail stores stay closed on Mondays, for instance. And more and more offices are exploring alternative scheduling such as working four ten-hour days instead of five eight-hour days.

Fine-dining restaurants are great at fine-tuning business hours. When times are good, you'll see many eateries open for lunch to capture additional business. When the economy goes down, many will discontinue lunch service or close on Mondays.

High-end retail businesses may discontinue regular hours altogether and switch to a "by appointment only" operating model, drastically reducing their hours. Scaling back business hours can save on labor, utilities, materials costs, and wear and tear on your facility.

One retail chain that has mastered the art of curtailing hours is the closeout retailer Tuesday Morning. The 850-store company does not keep a regular schedule and closes for all periods that are likely to be slow—for instance, last year the chain was closed for the entire week that contained the Fourth of July holiday. The closures only build customer interest and give the shopping experience a more exclusive, bargain-hunting feel.

MERCHANDISING

Most small retailers arrange their own store windows and in-store displays, a highly labor-intensive undertaking. They do their own inventory tracking as well, and then expend time placing orders with vendors when merchandise levels fall.

This is not how the big chains do it, though. They push these tasks off onto their major vendors in a process known as "vendor-managed inventory." In this scenario, you and the vendor use common software that allows the vendor to see when your inventory is getting low, without even having to call or email you.

When stocks fall to an agreed-upon level, the vendor ships or brings more product to the store. Merchandisers working for the vendor may also set up merchandise displays. Using a vendor-managed inventory approach can give you better-looking displays without paying more, as vendors may offer this service as a perk to stay competitive with similar vendors. You may have a tough time getting vendors to take this on for you at the start, but with even a couple of months' operating experience you could approach your vendors. If they're managing inventory for other accounts, they might be willing to add you to their program.

Think of operating costs as rocks and ruts in the road to your startup's success. The more operating costs you can reduce or remove, the smoother your road to profitability becomes, and the faster you can get there.

Chapter 11

PURCHASING

I once had the educational experience of interviewing the owner of a thriving Southern California hardware-store chain. The owner was a longtime retailer who took pride in showing me around one of his sparkling, clean stores.

Down a wide back aisle were a row of "dump" bins—large bins that hold seasonal or sale merchandise. He proudly pointed me to the bin he said held the best item in the store, a small, bright-yellow plastic flashlight that sold for $1.

I was a little baffled. Cheap flashlights that went for only $1? I asked him why this was the best item.

"Oh, I bought them for a penny each!" he proclaimed.

If you want to know how the big retail chains stay in business, this is how: They buy on very wide margins, whenever possible. Often, businesses will have some core products they need to have to serve their customers that have fairly narrow margins. They compensate for this problem by finding those $1 flashlight buys. They look for situations in which they can purchase an item they can sell for 100 times—or even 300 times—what they paid.

Big margins equal big profits. A good business owner looks to constantly drive down the cost of goods sold. You want to buy goods for rock-bottom prices, so you can mark them up high and make enough to stay in business.

Bargain Hunting 101

Start with the basic philosophy that you are always looking for a cheaper vendor, a lower-priced product of similar quality, and a better deal. Institute regular reviews of your purchase prices. Watch for price hikes from vendors—that should always trigger a review to see if a lower-priced vendor can be found.

Here are ten good ways a startup can cut purchasing costs:

1. **Closeouts.** All around the world, retailers make mistakes. They order far more orange sweaters than women turn out to want. Manufacturers make them, too, deciding to do huge production runs of merchandise hoping to land a big retail account that never materializes. Or a manufacturer decides to stop making an item and doesn't have enough left to sell to its major accounts, but the company still has a few pallets they must clear out of the warehouse to free up space for the new model.

People are human and make mistakes—then, they've got to figure out how to unload those problems, often taking pennies on the dollar just to be rid of the goods. Otherwise, the manufacturer or retailer has to pay for warehouse space to house its boo-boos, on top of the lost revenue from bad planning.

Where does all this surplus merchandise end up? It used to turn up at closeout shows, live industry events where suppliers would gather at a convention center to unload their excess goods. This is where my hardware-chain owner used to go with his retailer buddies to buy items like those $1 flashlights.

At this point, the live closeout show is dying out in favor of online merchandise closeout websites. Wholesale lots of closeout goods turn up both on the big, well-known resale websites such as eBay and its subsidiary Overstock.com and on specialty websites such as Liquidation.com and CloseoutsWorld. These sites offer surplus merchandise in a wide variety of retail categories, sold by the pallet, case, or truckload. Be on watch for specialists in particular merchandise types, too, and for regular wholesalers who have a "close-outs" tab on their websites.

2. **Auctions.** Some surplus merchandise is sold at auctions. Place a minimum bid on a

merchandise lot no one else wants, and you might end up with a serious deal. Besides checking online auction websites, search for auctioneers in your area that hold in-person merchandise auctions. In Boswell, Indiana, for example, the Boswell Trade Center auctions surplus goods of all kinds every Tuesday. If you think you can't find the type of merchandise you need at an auction or on close-out sites, think again—they sell everything from toys, candy, and apparel to knives, motorcycles, and the latest tech devices.

3. **Bulk buys.** It can be hard to buy in large quantities when you're first launching your business, as you may not have the capital, the storage space, or a good sense of customer demand yet. But as soon as you begin to grow, start looking into buying bigger amounts. Many vendors offer discounts for bulk purchases. Ask your vendors what thresholds you need to hit to start paying less for your merchandise. Then, get to that purchasing level as fast as you can. Every dime you save on bulk buying goes straight to the bottom line as additional profit.

4. **Buying groups and co-ops.** One of the major disadvantages of running a small, independent business is that you don't have the

buying power of the big chains. They get better bulk-buying deals by purchasing vast quantities from vendors. You can overcome this problem by joining an independent buying group. In buying groups, many indie retailers band together to make group purchases. There are independent buying groups for many types of retailing, including the Independent Pharmacy Buying Group, the Independent Stationers, and MEGA Group for home-goods stores.

While some buying groups make no demands on how you brand your store, others align under a common brand—a well-known example is Ace Hardware. In some groups, the store owners may all be shareholders or owners of the buying group, sharing equally in its success and in the risks of its purchases.

5. **Vendor consolidation.** Here's another way the big chains save money that small retailers often miss: As you start up your business, your buying may be disorganized and spread amongst dozens of vendors. That leads to higher prices because vendors offer breaks if you buy more through them. Large chains do annual vendor consolidation initiatives to try to reduce the number of their suppliers and score better pricing.

Take a page from their book and periodically review your vendor list. Concentrating your buying on fewer vendors can help you cut purchase prices. Do a vendor review and ask existing vendors whether they carry some of the other products you buy elsewhere, or offer similar products. If you can drop some vendors to do more business with a select few, they should be willing to offer you better pricing.

The bonus: When vendors catch wind that you're doing a review with an eye to consolidation, some may come up with better pricing for you in order to keep your business. They don't want to be on the list of vendors that get cut.

6. **SKU consolidation.** A SKU is a stock-keeping unit—in other words, one single item you stock in your store. For instance, if you carry women's T-shirts in three colors each in small, medium, and large sizes, that is nine SKUs of merchandise.

It's a common problem that new retailers carry too many items, not all of which are profitable. You have goods sitting in the stockroom or on the shelves and not moving. As quickly as you can, analyze what your best movers are, and identify your best profit items. At the same time, identify slow-movers and low-margin items, and eliminate them. The more SKUs you carry, the greater your purchasing costs.

7. **Down-stocking.** Keep stores as minimally stocked as possible while still appearing full, especially if you're not in a position to buy enough volume to qualify for bulk buy pricing. Use shallower racks so that the store looks full with fewer items on display. If merchandise is piling up in the stockroom, that represents money that is tied up in your business and can't be used for other business goals—and the merchandise isn't even out where customers can see it!

8. **Online sourcing.** It has never been easier to compare pricing between vendors or find international sources of cheap goods. The major web portal Alibaba is one of the biggest business-to-business sourcing marketplaces online, allowing you to easily check prices on goods being produced in countries around the world. You may find a similar or even identical item at a lower price elsewhere.

9. **Early-pay discounts.** Even on day one, there is always at least one way you can pay less— many vendors offer a discount for paying early or on time. Be sure to track these dates and save every dime you can by paying

promptly. If your vendors aren't offering one, contact them and ask if they'd be willing to grant you a discount for paying quickly.

10. **Near-sourcing.** While the conventional wisdom says goods made overseas are always cheaper, that's not always true. Especially in this age of rising fuel costs, shipping goods in from abroad involves steep transportation costs. Research whether a closer vendor might be found with similar pricing, and if there is one, your overall cost for those goods will go down. This doesn't necessarily mean you need to find a vendor in your town—if you're a Texas-based retailer buying from China and you find a replacement vendor in Mexico, this can represent a huge transportation savings.

CASE STUDY: A BUSINESS BUILT ON LOW-COST GOODS

In 2002, Notre Dame students Xavier Helgesen, Christopher "Kreece" Fuchs, and Jeff Kurtzman went searching for a low-cost business they could start. The trio came to focus on a product that was right under their noses and could be purchased at a low cost: obsolete textbooks. Their company, Better World Books, gave students and colleges a way to resell old textbooks to other learning institutions around the globe that still use them. Since obsolete textbooks are considered nearly worthless by the discarding institution, sellers were happy to get anything for them—and happy to give Indiana-based Better World a cut of the sale price.

The business takes a small cut of the sales price and essentially pays nothing for its inventory of millions of books, which are shipped to its warehouses on consignment. The company now sells more than five million books annually.

As you can see, there are many options to consider before you pay full rip for an item. Keep an eye out for bargains, and you can save a bundle on purchasing.

Chapter 12

TRANSPORTATION AND SHIPPING

business idea can sometimes look solidly profitable—until you factor in the cost of getting goods from where they're made to you and from there on to your customer. Likewise, a consulting business can sound terrific until you realize you'll be driving hundreds of miles to client sites and paying for your own gas and vehicle upkeep.

Transportation and shipping costs tend to not come in a steady dribble through the year, so it's easy to overlook them in your drive to keep costs low. Don't make this mistake! Constantly seek opportunities to slash these expenses. Remember, these niggling costs are standing between you and higher profits.

THIRTEEN WAYS TO CUT TRANSPORTATION AND SHIPPING COSTS

1. **Reduce use.** The first line of defense is to see if you could avoid transportation or shipping cost completely. For instance, examine your business trips and in-person customer calls to see if they could be curtailed. Could customers pick up goods in-store instead of having them mailed out? Might some customers come to your office instead? Could some meetings be held on Skype instead of in person? Keep looking for opportunities to eliminate these costs.

2. **Make customers pay.** In some business sectors such as mail-order retail, customers accept the addition of shipping charges to their bill without a blink. Test the waters to see how much resistance you get to the idea of tacking on shipping charges when you invoice customers.

   Also explore whether you can mark up shipping when you charge customers and make a profit on it. This is a method employed by many catalog retailers to add additional profit to their bottom line. *Remember, the customer doesn't know what you pay for shipping.*

3. **Drop-ship.** Rather than taking delivery of goods from manufacturers, consider becoming

a drop-ship vendor. In this model, you don't stock goods in your store or stash them in your garage but instead order them *for* the customer and get the manufacturer or wholesaler to ship them directly *to* the customer. This often results in a lower shipping charge as goods travel a shorter distance. Drop-shipping also saves on storage and labor costs since you never handle or store the merchandise.

4. **Consolidate.** There is often a lot of waste in both travel and deliveries. For instance, if salespeople are going on two monthly sales trips at different times of the month, it could save the cost of one plane ticket home to have them schedule one longer road trip with two stops instead. If three trucks are making deliveries on different routes daily, see if those routes could be reorganized so that only two trucks are needed. If sales staff make in-person calls, make sure prospects in one neighborhood are all scheduled for the same day.

If you are getting office supplies delivered to your place of business, get organized and place fewer orders to reduce expenses. For instance, my local Staples will deliver free to my home office for any order over $50, so I make a point of waiting until I have at least that much to order, to avoid a delivery fee.

5. **Get efficient.** The major retailers and shippers are masters at squeezing out shipping

inefficiencies. Take a page from their books if you are operating your own vehicles. For instance, UPS noted in its 2010 sustainability report that redesigning delivery routes to eliminate left turns—which often require gas-wasting idling at traffic lights—saved twenty million miles of driving in a single year. Retailer Staples installed devices on its delivery trucks that limited their speed to sixty miles per hour—and reported a 20 percent improvement in fuel economy. Devices installed in 2009 to automatically shut off trucks if they idled too long saved the company $3 million in a single year in the United States alone. Obviously, the savings of a small business won't be on this scale, but they can still be meaningful.

6. **Pack light.** Have you ever gotten a big package delivered, only to find it consisted mostly of packing peanuts and, finally, just one small product buried deep in the middle? Customers hate overpackaging, and it creates waste and additional shipping cost by adding more weight and size to your packages. This doesn't have to happen—there are better solutions out there for packing efficiently.

For instance, in food service the Pactiv packing system requires all vendors to use the same size packages. This makes it possible to fill up trucks completely, eliminating wasted space inside trucks and improving shipping efficiency.

Often, the problem is that small retailers buy only a few sizes of shipping boxes to use, and then shoehorn all products into them simply to avoid having to manage additional box sizes. This is why we end up with the tiny product inside the big box. Technology has caught up to this problem, though—Packsize makes all-in-one box machines capable of creating a custom-sized box to fit each outgoing shipment, allowing retailers and shippers to make each package the minimum size needed.

Besides shipping boxes, your business can also save by favoring products that come in less bulky packaging, so more units can fit in a box or pallet. Many of the biggest retailers, including Walmart, are pressuring manufacturers to make more streamlined packages— ride their coattails and order in bulk bins rather than individually wrapped packages, or switch to vendors offering less packaged goods.

7. **Shop for gas.** I used to rag on my father constantly because of his obsession with gas prices. On driving trips to visit me, he would carefully note the price of gas at each station— then make a point of stopping at the cheapest one on the way home. You won't think this focus is silly if you have a lot of business trips

or deliveries to make, though, because gas prices are high and forecast to stay that way, and gas charges add up fast.

If you have substantial travel in your business for meetings or deliveries, seek out gas discount programs. The Costco warehouse chain and Safeway grocery stores are just two of many big chains offering discounted gas deals to shoppers.

8. **Backhaul.** When trucks make deliveries, they then must return to the manufacturing plant or warehouse empty—unless an enterprising entrepreneur contracts to use that return-trip or backhaul capacity to ship its goods at a discount. The Internet has made it easier to locate backhaul trucks that might be going where you need deliveries made, too—websites such as 123Loadboard and Load Authority in the United States and Shiply in Europe help vendors and retailers coordinate and find bargain-priced backhaul capacity.

9. **Negotiate.** Shipping charges are not standardized, nonnegotiable costs. If you are going to be doing a volume of shipping, the shipping companies will compete for your business. Get more than one quote, and play the carriers off against each other to get the best deal. Getting a discount on shipping can deliver

serious savings, as one e-commerce company recently discovered. Here's the story of how its owners designed their entire business model to drive down shipping costs:

CASE STUDY: PETFLOW

In 2009, Joe Speiser and Alex Zhardanovsky were looking to start a new online business and gravitated to the pet industry. Yes, famous dot-com flameouts such as Pets.com seemed to prove that it wasn't a good sector to try selling online. But when the pair researched what had gone wrong in the past, they found key problems in Pets.com's business model, particularly when it came to shipping.

In a two-hour interview with former Pets.com CEO Julie Wainwright, Zhardanovsky learned that the company had carried 15,000 items—everything from dog food to collars to impulse purchases like beds and dog treats. The model was designed to inspire one-time orders rather than recurring business.

Armed with this insight, PetFlow went another direction, carrying just 4,000 varieties of pet food available for automatic, monthly delivery, including many hard-to-find brands. This recurring-purchase model allowed Zhardanovsky to present a strong case to shippers that his new company would be a steady source of business.

With just a couple of months' track record that showed increasing sales, PetFlow was able to negotiate substantial shipping discounts from FedEx, paying roughly 60 percent of what a consumer would pay to ship a single item. The price break allowed PetFlow to offer customers pet-food prices similar to what they'd pay in a retail store. PetFlow charges just $4.95 for shipping of purchases under $60, a low cost customers happily pay for the convenience of not having to run to the grocery store when they're out of pet food, or heft heavy sacks of food into the house.

"We approached FedEx almost like an investor," says Zhardanovsky. "We said, 'The money you're giving us in the form of volume discounts that we may not yet be entitled to, we will use to acquire new customers, and that is new shipments you are going to get.'"

Launched in 2010, PetFlow's model was an instant hit with customers, bringing in $1 million a month in sales by the end of the first year. PetFlow drove sales in part by incentivizing customers to order larger quantities at once—a thirty-pound bag of dog food, say, instead of two fifteen-pound bags—in order to reap even more shipping savings. The company now ships over 1.5 million pounds of dog food monthly and saw $29 million in 2012 sales.

10. **Near-source.** Here's where going green can really save you money. If you source a product from overseas, research whether you might find a similar product at a similar price closer to home. If you can switch from a vendor in China to one in Mexico, the difference in shipping costs can be meaningful. You might pay slightly more for an item made nearer and still come out ahead.

11. **Consolidate vendors.** There is a basic math to shipping: When you order just a few items from many vendors, it's less efficient to ship those goods from many places than it would be to place a few large orders from a smaller vendor list. Endeavor to consolidate shipments from fewer warehouses or vendors to cut shipping costs.

12. **Pay only for the speed you need.** PetFlow's Zhardanovsky quickly learned that in some regions of the United States, selecting two-day ground delivery from a particular carrier fairly reliably got packages to their destination in one day simply due to the vagaries of how that carrier schedules its planes and trucks. He recommends sending test packages various distances to see where you might save more money on shipping—and make more margin—by charging the customer for one-day delivery but in reality shipping two-day ground. If the system fails you, you can always refund the extra shipping fee that customer paid, but in the meanwhile you could reap savings on many packages' shipping fees.

When your business is the one ordering supplies, keep the shipping rules in mind, too. Strive to leave enough time to order goods on the "slow boat" to get the lowest rates. Avoid paying for pricey rush or overnight shipping.

13. **Hire a coordinator.** In some business types, transportation and shipping costs are so burdensome that it makes sense to hire someone to do nothing but hunt and eliminate these expenses. Having one person in the office make all the travel plans, for instance, can allow the company to take advantage of bulk-travel discounts that might not be available if individual members of the sales staff each book their own trips.

Zhardanovsky points out that you get just as much service from shippers for the lower price.

"The guy who delivers my package has no idea what I paid for it," he says. "It's shipped just like the package another customer paid twice as much for. So you should try to save as much as you can in shipping."

Chapter 13

Labor

E ven if you start an e-commerce business or form a one-person consulting firm, at some point you will need help. Some tasks you won't know how to do; others you may want to off-load simply because you don't enjoy them.

Many entrepreneurs make the mistake of being unwilling to delegate. Remember that your time is limited and you should focus on where you can make the most impact on the business—it might be new-product design, or maybe sales. Off-loading other tasks that don't directly drive new business is a smart move that should help you grow the business faster.

That said, labor costs can quickly drain a startup of cash if you're not careful. Too many entrepreneurs make the mistake of hiring full-time employees before the business is making enough to cover their salaries. Your goal as a startup owner should be to postpone making permanent hires for as long as possible.

Fortunately, there are plenty of ways to get the work you need done on the cheap.

Thirteen Ways to Save on Labor

1. **Automation.** If you have administrative work that needs doing, see if there isn't a piece of software that could execute the task or make it easier to do. This will eliminate the need for help with some tasks.

2. **Unpaid internship.** If you are thinking about hiring someone but the job requires some training, you may be able to structure an unpaid internship, especially if the candidate is a recent college graduate. But be warned: the US Department of Labor's rules governing unpaid internships are strict, and lawsuits are on the rise from former unpaid interns who claim that their internship should have been paid. Avoid costly legal trouble and make sure your unpaid internship meets the legal requirements.

   To qualify as an unpaid internship, the Department of Labor requires the following:

   - There is a clear understanding up front that the internship is unpaid
   - The training given the intern is similar to what she would receive in an educational environment

- The internship must benefit the intern, giving her new knowledge
- The intern's work does not displace the work of any paid employees
- The intern works under close staff supervision
- The intern is not necessarily entitled to a paid job at the end of the internship
- None of the intern's work directly benefits the business—she may only undertake practice or training activities

For many businesses, the inability to put the intern to work on any projects that directly help the business may rule out this idea. But this can be a way to train a young worker and make sure there's a fit before making a paid hire.

3. **Paid internship.** Paid interns must be paid at least the minimum wage and overtime pay for any hours worked beyond a standard forty-hour week under the Fair Labor Standards Act. A paid intern can work on projects that benefit the business. As with an unpaid internship, a paid internship can give you a chance to try out a young worker at a lower pay level and on a temporary basis.

4. **Barter.** As noted in the Market Research chapter, you might trade services with other professionals who have skills your business needs. For instance, I've written website copy

for designers and webmasters who then did design or coding work on my blog as an even trade.

5. **Offer equity.** Many tech startups have bootstrapped on a tiny budget by offering key programmers a stake in the company in lieu of pay. If the programmers believe you are building the next Facebook, they may be willing to put in some time with you gratis on the gamble that their efforts will make them rich later. Be aware that you are giving up a slice of your ownership of the company when you do this, and make sure you retain the level of ownership you want.

6. **Hire a freelancer.** With a little local networking, you can find qualified freelance contractors in a wide variety of fields. Your local chamber of commerce is usually a good first stop, particularly if you want someone you can meet with in person. One big advantage is that freelancers are not bound by federal wage and hour laws and are free to negotiate whatever rate you mutually decide. Biggest savings here, though, lie in the employment tax, disability, workers comp, health care, vacation, and other fringe benefits you won't have to pay. (See the "Taxes" chapter for a primer on determining if a worker is a freelancer or an employee.)

7. **Using freelancer websites.** In the past decade, online platforms have sprung up that bring freelance workers together with employers looking for low-cost help. Especially if you are comfortable hiring people from Third World countries who may not have strong English skills, you may be able to hire help at amazingly low rates through these online marketplaces.

There are both advantages and drawbacks to hiring through some of these platforms. Some platforms help manage your relationships with the freelancers. For instance, some will hold your funds in an escrow account and only release them to the freelancer when a job is done to your satisfaction. Others offer tracking software that monitors whether a freelancer is actually working on your tasks during the hours they bill.

On the dark side, most quality freelancers wouldn't be caught dead bidding on jobs on these sites. The freelancers tend to be either new to their field and looking to build their portfolio or from outside the United States. Complaints about unfinished or poor-quality work performed by contractors obtained through mass platforms such as these are rampant.

Be sure to carefully check the portfolio, referrals, and credentials of freelancers you seek to hire. Consider assigning a small project first to make sure you like a freelancer's work before committing more time and money to a bigger project.

Here are a few of the largest freelance marketplaces:

- **99designs.** This is one of the biggest sites for hiring a freelance website or graphic designer.
- **Amazon Mechanical Turk.** The retail giant's freelance platform is known for slicing work up into small units dubbed Human Intelligence Tasks, or HITs. This system allows you to outsource even minor, quick tasks.
- **Craigslist.** If you need someone local to come on-site, Craigslist allows you to advertise to freelancers in your specific city.
- **Elance.** This large site offers freelance work to programmers, marketers, administrators, and creative professionals.
- **FlexJobs.** This site is known for aggregating better-quality contract opportunities from scores of other online job websites and also offers exclusive listings of its own.
- **Freelancer.** This site boasts it is the world's largest outsourcing market, attracting freelancers in tech, design, writing, mobile, sales, marketing, and many other categories.
- **GetACoder.** A leader in offering freelance web help.

- **Guru.com.** With seventeen different freelancer categories and an emphasis on vetting credentials, this is one of the largest wide-spectrum freelancer platforms.
- **oDesk.** Nine broad categories of freelancers are found here, including business-service professionals such as accountants, transcribers, and web developers.
- **People Per Hour.** A wide variety of job types are listed here with an emphasis on technology skills.

8. **Hire a student.** High school and college students need money and are always looking for flexible-hour jobs or freelance gigs that can be done outside of school hours. When I started my freelance writing business in 2005, I hired a teenager from my local high school's digital design class to design my website and serve as webmaster. He did great work at low rates, and the relationship lasted eighteen months.

Another startup founder who relied on freelancers is Jason Glaspey. When he started his web-based diet site, Paleo Plan, in 2009, he saved money by hiring students from the local branch of a private college chain, The Art Institutes, to do design work on a project basis for $10–$15 per hour. Glaspey says students are excited to work in e-commerce, compared with the usual positions students get offered, such as minimum-wage fast-food gigs.

His advice for hiring students? "Don't look for one student who can do everything you need. Break it up so you only need four hours a week from each one, and the task is something in their chosen industry."

9. **Bring the family.** Hiring family members can have some tax advantages, and they may agree to modest wages, particularly if they are your children. But be wary as having family members in the business can lead to problems, too. Many small businesses went down the drain while family members stood around the store squabbling with each other. If you do hire family, make sure you are crystal clear on your expectations of the work they will do and the pay they will receive.

10. **Hire temporary workers.** Even if you think you may need a full-time worker, don't make a permanent hire right off. "Temp-to-perm" hires are common now and a good avenue for start-ups. Try out a likely candidate for three to six months. With a temporary worker, you won't have the obligations of a full-time hire. Temp hires also allow you to staff up for a busy season or specific project and then easily end the employment whenever your need ends.

11. **Hire part-time workers.** If you need steady hours from a worker, consider starting with a part-time hire. Part-time workers won't

require the costly fringe benefits of a permanent, full-time hire.

12. **Offer flexible schedules.** You can often get skilled pros to work for less if you will give them the one thing Corporate America won't: flexibility. Let them work remotely on their own schedule if possible. Don't be a micromanager who needs workers warming a chair right in front of him—that lowers productivity, anyway.

13. **Hire a special person.** If you do need an employee, explore whether there are any federal or state hiring-stimulus programs that might help reduce your costs. For instance, the federal Hiring Incentives to Restore Employment (HIRE) Act created tax breaks for employers that hired workers in 2010 who had been unemployed for at least sixty days. There are also programs that provide assistance to employers hiring the disabled or veterans (or disabled veterans). These incentives come and go, so be sure to research available assistance programs if you plan to hire someone whose special circumstances might entitle you to government aid.

TIPS FOR HIRING RIGHT

One of the toughest jobs a new business owner faces is identifying the best candidates to hire. If you come out of a corporate environment, you may not have hired before. Much time and money is often wasted because inexperienced owners tend to make bad hires based on gut feelings, on impulse, or out of convenience. Having to train multiple workers to fill one position drains your resources and can cost your business critical momentum when you are trying to ramp up sales.

For instance, I once talked to a business owner who had hired her next-door neighbor to work in her senior-care business, simply because they struck up a conversation and the neighbor expressed interest in the position! This isn't how you hire the best candidate for the job.

Here is a five-step quick guide to making a great first hire:

1. **Write a job description.** This will help you get a clear picture of the skills you need in the position and help you find a qualified candidate. If you aren't sure, try searching for similar jobs on Monster.com or other big job websites and see what other employers ask for in a similar position.

2. **Network.** Before placing a job ad that may have you wading through hundreds of resumes, make everyone you know aware that you are hiring. For instance, when Rick and Lisa Roth needed to hire the first two auto mechanics to oversee their Phoenix-based do-it-yourself car-repair shop, U Fix It

Automotive, they asked around at local auto-parts stores. They were able to find both a seasoned senior mechanic and an experienced service associate without having to advertise.

3. **Interview to the job description.** Interviewing candidates can be nerve-wracking. Often, employers end up just shooting the breeze with applicants instead of asking hard questions to find out more about their interest and qualifications. Have your job description in hand and ask specific questions about their knowledge and training to discover if they are a fit for your position.

4. **Hire to your culture.** Do you run a casual office where staffers wear shorts and bring their dogs? If a candidate comes in a three-piece suit, he or she is probably not for you. More importantly, if you expect all employees to feel empowered to solve problems but this candidate seems to lack that drive and initiative, he or she is probably not a fit. It's often said that you can teach a task but can't change a worker's attitude. Hire someone with the right attitude, and you can teach this person how to do the tasks you need.

5. **Find out what they want.** It's important to know why applicants are applying for your

position. Do they really hate this kind of work but can't find anything in their chosen field? Are they going back to school or moving away in a few months? Try to get them to talk about their motivations. The ideal candidate has a stable personal life and a genuine interest in your type of business.

If you feel hiring isn't your strength, consider enlisting a human-resource professional's help in vetting candidates. An impartial outsider's view may help you identify a better candidate than you could on your own.

Chapter 14

FINANCING

With the exception of setting up a bare-bones e-commerce business, most businesses need cash to get off the ground. Maybe you have some saved up that you can spend to get your business going. For instance, when she launched her women's undergarment company, Spanx—which today tops $1 billion in valuation—founder Sara Blakely budgeted $5,000 for her startup because that was what she had in the bank.

Some business types have higher startup costs, though. For instance, it's difficult to open a sit-down restaurant for less than $500,000 in any major city. Where can you get the cash? There are a limited number of options, and some of them come with fat interest costs.

Since late 2008, it's been difficult even for established business owners to get a bank loan, and interest rates are high. Startups are usually shut out entirely at traditional banks as too risky, unless you're opening a unit of a brand-name franchise. In that case, the franchisor might help you get a loan. Otherwise, this is an unlikely and costly option.

There are only four basic ways for a business to get money:

- Fund it with your own cash

- Get grant money

- Hand out shares of equity in the company in exchange for cash

- Borrow the funds and incur debt

Here is a look at the best options in each of these categories:

Cash

Self-fund. Too few entrepreneurs consider simply saving up the money they need. When it's your cash, you'll watch every dime—it's a natural curb on overspending. And investing your own cash means that the monthly revenue your company needs to break even is lower, thanks to the lack of interest payments on debt. You also keep all the ownership of the business, so you're in the best shape to grow and reap all the benefits of the business's success yourself.

Liquidate assets. If you have a second home, boat, valuable jewelry, or other nonessential assets, consider selling them to generate your startup cash. You won't have time to use them while you're ramping up your business anyway, and finding the cash will save you from racking up interest payments that could hobble your startup out of the gate.

Grants

The federal government gives few direct grants to small businesses except in the area of technology research and commercialization. The Small Business Innovation Research/Small Business Technology Transfer (SBIR/SBTT) program has funded nearly $27 billion in small-business research through more than 112,000 separate awards. SBIR money can be vital to launching a tech-focused business. Currently, eleven different federal agencies participate in the SBIR program.

The program has three phases. In the first one, up to $150,000 for six months of research is awarded to approved small businesses to help establish whether a new technology is feasible and has commercial potential. In the second phase, up to $1 million is awarded for a two-year advanced research period. In phase three, SBIR may award more money or help facilitate private-sector investment.

States are increasingly interested in making business grants as well and may fund a wider range of business types. A notable example is InvestMaryland, the state's effort to invest at least $70 million in state-based small and startup businesses over fifteen years. Smaller business-grant programs include Virginia's Small Business Investment Grant program announced in mid-2012, which will pledge 10 percent of needed growth funds to qualified businesses, up to $1.5 million in all.

Business-grant programs come and go as various objectives arise in a particular region. Local grants or tax incentives might be offered to lure businesses to an economically depressed area of a city, stimulate the establishment of a technology or biotech hub, or assist minority business owners, for instance.

Investigate state and local grant opportunities in your own locale to learn what's currently available.

Equity options
Find a big-time investor. In particular industries, such as health care and technology, startups often turn to qualified wealthy investors, either individual "angel" investors or venture-capital firms. These "accredited" or qualified investors have been vetted by the Securities and Exchange Commission (SEC) as having experience in investing and a net worth of at least $1 million or $200,000 in annual income. Equity investment means the investors give you money with no immediate monthly payments or interest. Instead, they acquire a partial ownership in your firm. These investors are hoping the business grows in value and their stake in the company will be worth more in three to five years, at which point they hope to cash out and take home their profits.

Finding a big investor sounds great, but there are a few harsh realities here:

- **Few succeed.** The National Venture Capital Association reports that only 1,000 businesses received first-time venture capital in 2010, out of nearly six million American businesses. So it's a real needle-in-a-haystack thing.

- **Control may be lost.** What many startup owners don't realize is that most equity investors won't settle for 5 percent of your business—they're going to want a big stake, often more than 50 percent. They may well want a seat on your board and a voice in major decisions the business makes. Also, you run the risk that you are sacrificing future billions in revenue that will now belong to that investor. Many owners aren't interested in giving up either the control of their business or the upside potential that might make them rich in the future.

- **Exit must be considered.** Once investors own half your business, they will want to be able to get their money back out at some point. Often, this means the business must refinance with debt, be sold, or raise money in a public stock offering. If your vision is that you want to continue running and controlling your business for the foreseeable future, equity investors may not be a good fit.

- **Shares may be sold to small investors.** With the passage of the 2012 Jumpstart Our Business Startups (JOBS) Act, a new fundraising avenue opened up to startups. The rules of this act allow businesses to sell equity shares of their company privately to many small investors without having to file reports with the SEC. The act also opened the door for businesses to publicly advertise and promote their small equity offerings, where in the past only accredited investors could be shown the top-secret prospectus describing the investment opportunity.

Here's a quick look at some of the important provisions in this new law that affect startups seeking equity investors:

- Businesses can sell shares worth the greater of $2,000 or 5 percent of an investor's annual income or net worth to investors with less than $100,000 in net worth

- Investors with more than $100,000 in annual income or net worth can buy shares up to 10 percent of their net worth

- You can raise up to $1 million in any one-year period from small investors

- Previously, if you had more than 500 private shareholders, your business would have had to file financial disclosures with the SEC. The JOBS Act increases that threshold to 2,000 as long as fewer than 500 of those shareholders are not accredited investors.

In reaction to this change, new online platforms, such as MicroVentures and CircleUp, are springing up that aim to connect entrepreneurs with small investors. These sites help promote your equity offer and facilitate your investor deals, taking a small percentage of the funding amount for their trouble.

These online funding platforms are small now but growing quickly. Founded in 2009, MicroVentures facilitated $1.2 million in fundraising in 2011, says founder Bill Clark. That grew to $13 million in equity-funding deals completed in 2012. The site has more than 8,000 investors and business owners signed up, and Clark reports that a typical equity deal is for $500,000. MicroVentures charges 5 percent of any funds raised through the platform as its commission.

By mid-2012, Clark expected the implementation of the JOBS Act's loosened advertising restrictions to bring more investors to crowdfunding platforms. One intriguing advantage here is that the time to complete a deal is short and getting shorter as word spreads about crowdfunded equity.

"When we started out, it was three months for the first deal," he says. "Now, the average is one month."

In a twist on this model, AngelList and other platforms charge a fee to help startups meet investors but then leave you to structure your own investor deals. This area of startup finance is just developing in the wake of the JOBS Act, so investigate what new options may be emerging if you're looking for help finding a pool of small investors.

DEBT OPTIONS

1. **Trade or vendor credit.** This technique won't get you cash. But if you need money to purchase merchandise, it's worth inquiring to see if vendors will send you merchandise on credit. Often, they'll agree—they are always hot to land new clients. Vendors frequently offer retailers at least a month in which to pay for goods. That gives you breathing space to sell the goods. If you succeed, you could pay vendors with customers' money rather than your own. This is exactly how all the big retail chains preserve their cash.

2. **Microloans.** Many small businesses need only a small amount to get started—perhaps a few thousand dollars. Traditional banks are uninterested in making these sort of small loans, particularly to unproven entrepreneurs. Specialized microlenders are filling this gap. In 2010, a study by the Aspen Institute, a microenterprise-focused nonprofit, found that the microlending sector included more than 750 microenterprise programs. More than 12,500 microloans were made, and the microloans outstanding that year topped $132 million. By keeping the amount of the loan small, you limit the amount of interest you will pay.

   While microloans got their start with India's Grameen Bank, they have become an increasingly important financing vehicle for US entrepreneurs seeking small loans. One of the largest US microlenders is Accion USA, which has provided more than $119 million in small loans since 1991.

   Microloans are commonly made to entrepreneurs within small support groups organized by the lender. The business owners assist each other in staying on track to pay off their loans. Microlenders often have a preference for assisting minority entrepreneurs or businesses operating in economically distressed areas.

3. **Peer loan.** This online lending method emerged around 2005 with websites such as Prosper.com and LendingClub. These sites allow businesses to borrow money from a large number of individual lenders, with the site aggregating their small contributions—$50 per lender is common—and serving as loan administrator. Rates vary widely, but if you have a good credit rating and an interesting business story to tell, you might get a loan at a modest rate on par with prevailing bank interest rates.

   On most of these platforms, you will need to obtain the entire loan amount you seek in order to receive the funding—otherwise, you get nothing. Monthly loan payments are required, just as with a traditional bank loan. If you're delinquent or fail to pay, it will damage your credit rating.

4. **Gift-funding sites.** These are like peer-lending sites but with a twist—the money you get isn't a loan. It's a donation you don't ever have to pay back. Interest rate: zero. Loan payments: zero.

   The best known of these sites is KickStarter, which began in 2009. On KickStarter and similar sites, entrepreneurs make a video that tells their story in a bid for funding. By KickStarter's rules, the funding must be used for a specific business project and cannot be for general business purposes. For instance, you might ask for money to open a store or manufacture a product.

The trick is that the money is not truly free. To entice bidders, entrepreneurs usually offer something in return. Often, it's product at wholesale prices. So the money does come at some cost.

If you have an exciting offer and a large social network to spread the word about your KickStarter campaign, this can be a very successful fundraising approach. Running a Kickstarter campaign can also serve as a great source of market research—you find out if consumers are really interested in your products, and if so, in which styles/colors—and you can offer bigger investors proof that your product does have a market.

For instance, in 2011, the design firm Minimal did a KickStarter campaign to get money to manufacture its new line of TikTok watches, which turn an iPod Nano into a wristwatch. Aiming to raise $15,000 for a first manufacturing run of the watches, Minimal found that techies were rabid for their design. The company ended up raising a staggering $940,000!

This was a double-edged sword—it was a great way to launch a new product and generated tons of buzz for the company, but at the same time it meant that Minimal ended up handing out a large quantity of its watches at below-retail price. On the plus side, the company got strong confirmation that its product was of high interest to consumers, and Minimal got huge media attention from the success of its campaign.

5. **Borrow from your home equity line of credit.** This used to be a highly popular method of business financing. Rates can be quite low—at the end of 2012, for instance, my own home equity line was only charging me 2.9 percent interest. But after the economy turned down in late 2008, the home equity picture changed drastically. Banks became far more skittish about offering home equity lines, "capping" many existing credit lines at whatever had already been borrowed out.

   Now, many homeowners have "underwater" mortgages, so there is no home equity built up that they can tap. In any case, borrowing out of your house to start a business isn't recommended—if your business tanks and you can't repay a home equity loan, you stand to lose your home as well as your livelihood.

6. **Cash out or borrow from your retirement fund.** This is another area where you should proceed with caution. Many entrepreneurs throughout the 1980s and 1990s did a maneuver known as ROBS, or rollovers as business

startups, to access their retirement funds to launch a business. There are finance companies that specialize in helping you set up this type of transaction.

ROBS works like this: First, you take the money in your existing retirement fund from your previous employer and roll the money into a new 401(k) plan you've set up for your new business. As this is now your company plan and you are the employer, you can borrow the money out tax-free and use it to run your business.

Or that's the theory, anyway. Since 2008, when it issued a formal warning about the issue, the IRS has taken an increasingly dim view of ROBS transactions. The agency has vowed to review all existing ROBS with an eye to disallowing them. If this happens to you, you would be required to put all of the money you borrowed back in the 401(k) plus interest and penalties—obviously, a huge financial blow for any company to take.

This is why financial experts recommend you simply borrow from your existing 401(k) and pay it back with interest—or better yet, cash it out entirely and pay the early-withdrawal penalties now.

In any case, borrowing from your retirement funds is a huge risk to be considered carefully. If your business doesn't succeed, you're not just without an income stream. Now, you have nothing to retire on, either.

7. **Equipment financing.** If the money you need is for the purchase of a piece of business equipment, such as company trucks, there are specialized lenders that can help. Rates for equipment loans can range from on par with bank rates and up, though, depending on your credit rating and the type of equipment involved. Many banks don't do equipment loans, so you may need to connect with a specialized lender. If you are opening a franchise, turn to your franchisor for help finding a low rate on equipment finance.

Better yet, consider leasing to reduce your needed capital. This approach has some tax advantages because you can deduct the payments as a business expense. It also means you don't have to worry about getting stuck with obsolete equipment—at the end of the lease, back it goes, and you can lease the newest model instead.

8. **Factoring.** If your business accepts credit cards or invoices its customers and there's a delay from when you bill to when you get paid, you might be able to get quick cash by using factoring. There are even emerging online platforms, such as The Receivables

Exchange, that will let you auction your receivables to get the best deal.

You'll hear this called a "factor loan," but in fact it's not a loan. What happens is a specialized lender purchases your outstanding receivables from you at a discount. The factoring firm gives you the remainder of your outstanding payments due right away, usually within a couple of days. Then, the factor lender waits for all those payments to roll in and keeps the difference.

Example: You sell $5,000 in receivables to a factor. The factor will discount your receivables on a formula that depends on your length of time in business, the quality of your clients (big retailers and government agencies are preferred), and past track record of defaulting payers. Many websites promise rates from a half a percent or so, but for startups with less history the rate will likely be higher—let's say it is 2 percent. That means the factor will pay you $4,900 and keep $100.

If you're strapped for cash, this will seem like manna from heaven, but watch out. The percentage you give up drains your business of needed cash. This can create a vicious cycle of reliance on factor lenders due to lack of cash flow.

9. **Loans from friends and family.** This is a common avenue for business fundraising, but it's one fraught with peril, and business-finance experts say it should be used only as a last resort. A relative may be willing to offer you a no-interest or low-interest loan, but think about how awkward that Thanksgiving table conversation is going to be if your business fails and you're unable to repay that person. Even a "free" loan from a relative usually comes with a lot of emotional strings attached. Think carefully about the implications for your personal life before accepting family money.

At the very least, if you do go this route, be professional about it—draw up a formal contract and carefully track your payments. Loan-tracking sites such as ZimpleMoney make this easy to do, and your loved ones will feel reassured when they can check and see the record of your repayments.

Bonus Idea: Zero-Interest Credit Cards

In general, credit cards are not a good way to finance your business due to the high interest rates. But they are one of the most common startup financing vehicles. A study commissioned by the Kauffman Foundation tracked business owners' credit-card usage in 2004 through 2006. They found nearly 60 percent of business owners used credit cards—and the businesses that went bust consistently had more credit-card debt than did surviving companies. The typical amount entrepreneurs have racked on their cards is rising, too—from $3,638 in 2004 to nearly $5,600 in 2006 among the businesses that closed.

However, there is a limited exception to the avoid-credit-cards rule. If you have good credit and get zero-interest credit card offers *and feel confident your company cash flow will allow you to pay off the amount you charge within the zero-interest period*—usually a year to eighteen months—this can be a useful vehicle for getting startup capital.

Just be careful to pay off your balance before interest starts being charged. Cards with initial zero-interest offers often charge sky-high interest once that initial period ends.

As you can see, no funding method is ideal, aside from having a pile of cash saved up. If you don't, be sure to factor any debt payments you'll have into your budget. You'll need to bring in enough revenue to service your debts in addition to paying all your other business overhead costs.

Chapter 15

CASH FLOW

O ften, businesses fail not because they haven't found customers but because of cash flow problems. In short, your business needs to have money flowing in faster than it's flowing out, or soon you'll be out of business. It's not unusual for a new business to see cycles of feast and famine, with some months doing well and others not. It's important to smooth out those lumps and bumps to ensure a steady flow of cash in order to avoid having to borrow to cover the lean months.

Many business owners don't have a focus on cash flow. It's easy to get excited as your startup gets those first few wins—I signed a big customer! This contract will bring in thousands!

Months later, when the payments haven't turned up, the excitement is gone. Your business has bills to pay, and now you don't have the money.

Why Cash Flow Matters

When businesses run short of cash, there are two common ways to address the problem: either you tap personal assets to keep the business afloat or the business must borrow.

Both of these moves spell trouble. You don't want to end up in personal bankruptcy, so draining the family checking account or racking up your personal credit card isn't advisable. Banks are uninterested in tiding you over—they like to lend to thriving businesses, not ones in financial trouble—so many new businesses are forced to use high-interest alternatives to stay afloat. Examples include:

- **Credit cards.** Plastic is the most common method of startup financing, used by 82 percent of business owners, according to a 2011 study from financial advisor Meredith Whitney Advisory Group. The high rates charged—currently ranging from about 14 percent upwards—just exacerbate the cash flow problem, often starting an inescapable cycle of shrinking cash and increasing debt service.

- **Purchase order (PO) loans.** This is a loan on a sale that is not yet complete. PO lenders give you money so you can manufacture or ship goods from a factory to a client. The PO loan is based on a signed purchase order from a major customer, such as a government agency or big retailer. The portion of income you'll give up here is even higher than it is with factoring (see the "Financing" chapter) since the risk to the lender is greater. In fact, the cut PO lenders take is so large that some won't work with you unless your business has at least 30 percent margins, in order to leave you with some profit after the lender's share is taken out.

- **Import-export loans.** If your customer is overseas or you are importing products from abroad, you might explore a loan from the Export-Import Bank of the United States, which specializes in this area. As with PO loans, rates will be high.

Using these sorts of high-cost loan vehicles, your business may be even more cash-starved a few months later. Quickly, your business comes to rely on debt to survive. Meanwhile, your business is hemorrhaging money—vital cash that should be going to growing your budding business. Instead, you need to manage your cash flow to make sure you always have money on hand to pay your bills.

In a nutshell: Cash flow problems cost your business money. You want to avoid them to keep your costs down.

There are three basic ways to improve your cash flow: You can get paid sooner, you can pay bills later, or you can cut costs. This whole book focuses on ways to cut costs, but below are a few specific tips to collect money faster, slow your cash outflow, and reduce your bills.

Get Paid Sooner

- **Have a credit application.** A big mistake many new owners make is extending credit based on their gut feelings about new clients. They extend credit to personal friends or relatives. Instead, create a credit application and make every customer seeking credit fill it out.

- **Research credit history.** Don't just take that credit application and smile—the next step is to investigate the customer's credit. Does he owe other merchants? Did he default on a loan? Is he behind on his mortgage? What is his overall credit rating? You can get answers to these questions by pulling a credit report from one of the three main credit-reporting agencies, Equifax, Experian, and TransUnion.

- **Create a credit policy—then, stick to it.** Instead of extending credit on a case-by-case basis, have a policy about the credit markers you want to see in order to grant credit. This makes it easier to say "no" to customers with shaky credit, as in: "Sorry, we're not able to extend credit to anyone with a rating below X level."

- **End credit for deadbeats.** Conduct a review of all existing clients who are buying on credit. Are they paying on time? If not, it's time to have a tactful conversation with them and let them know you're cutting them off. They need to pay cash in the future. One good strategy to avoid hard feelings is to make it about the business, not about them: "We've overextended ourselves on credit and need to cut back, sorry."

- **Require down payments.** This is especially key if your business delivers goods or services over a long time period. You don't want to wait months for a check while you are expending time and resources for a client. In my own freelance-writing business, I require 50 percent initial payments from new clients before starting work, for instance.

- **Create milestone payments.** Besides that down payment, if the project is long, create other trigger points for interim payments before completion. For instance, you might require 50 percent up front, 20 percent when half the work is completed, and the final 30 percent on completion.

- **Have a cutoff date for final payment.** One way contracts often go wrong is they fail to include a contingency for what happens if you complete your work, await the client's feedback . . . and the client disappears. You never get confirmation that your final work was satisfactory, so the final payment is never triggered. Include a drop-dead date in your contract by which time your final payment is due, as in, "Final payment is due on completion or within thirty days of turning in final work, whichever is soonest."

- **Hire a credit manager.** If telling customers to pay up fills you with dread, consider hiring a professional to handle this for you. Often, it helps to have a neutral third party calling on clients to deliver bad news about your turning them down or cutting off their credit—customers won't associate the credit decision directly with you and your business.

- **Carefully track outstanding payments.** You need a system such as QuickBooks or even a simple spreadsheet that allows you to see at a glance whose bill is overdue. Otherwise, payments will slip through the cracks.

- **Call on late payers immediately.** Many entrepreneurs feel uncomfortable calling late payers. This leads to months of delays in payments, as you hesitate to pick up the phone. Late payers should be contacted immediately, the day after their payment was due.

- **Offer an early-payment discount.** When you bill customers who are paying over time, offer them a small discount for paying immediately. Since we all love to save money, this may bring in some immediate cash.

- **Institute a late-payment penalty.** Motivate clients to pay on time by making it clear you will charge them a fee—2 percent or 3 percent a month, compounded, is common in many industries—if they don't pay on time.

- **Take a partial payment.** If the customer says that she's run into money troubles and can't pay, ask how much she could pay now. Take some up front and arrange a payment plan for the rest.

- **Settle the debt.** If a customer believes he'll never be able to pay the full amount, ask how much he can come up with, and get him to send it. Then, close the account. Carefully track any losses you take this way for goods delivered, as you can take a tax write-off for your cost of goods on the unpaid merchandise. (If you have a service business, unfortunately, there's no write-off.)

Pay Bills Later

- **Pay no bill before its time.** If you're sitting down once a month and paying all your business bills, you may be depriving the business of cash unnecessarily. Carefully note due dates on each bill and send payments out only when they are needed.

- **Switch payment plans.** Are some providers billing you quarterly or annually? See if you can switch to smaller monthly payments instead. This will help smooth out bumps in your cash flow, when you suddenly owe a big, occasional amount. It also keeps more of the payment in your pocket longer.

- **Ask for better vendor terms.** Once you've been in business a few months and have a track record of paying your bills, see if you can extend your terms from cash on delivery (C.O.D.) or net fifteen days to net thirty or forty-five, for instance. The longer you can wait to pay bills, the more time you have to bring in sales and generate cash for payments.

- **Pay bills late.** Some types of vendors don't charge late fees—my Internet and cable TV provider doesn't, for instance, nor does my electric utility company. If you need to hold a bill past its pay date to keep cash in your business account, look for bills you can pay late and not be penalized. You don't want to make a habit of this as it will hit your credit rating, but this is an occasional last-ditch strategy that can help with cash flow without costing you more.

THREE WAYS TO SAVE ON YOUR BILLS

You can often save some money in your own bill-paying cycle. This may impact your cash flow a bit, but the overall savings can be well worth it.

1. **Take advantage of early-pay discounts.** If vendors offer you a discount to pay now, do it if at all possible.

2. **Avoid late charges.** If you have credit debt or a vendor who you know will ding you if your payment is late, be sure not to miss those due dates. Interest payments and late fees waste your cash and add no value to the business.

3. **Question every line.** Don't pay bills on autopilot—scrutinize every charge on detail billings to make sure they are all legitimate and accurate. Root out mistakes and cancel services you aren't using. Don't accept bill increases without a fight—call and ask if you can be kept at the old rate.

Follow these steps and you should see more money stay in your business bank account. That will keep your business in better shape to withstand unexpected problems and will help you avoid any interest costs from debt incurred to cover cash flow problems.

Chapter 16

TAXES

There's nothing sadder than starting up an awesome, successful business only to find, come the following April, that you owe a staggering chunk of your budding business's revenue to your state and the IRS for taxes.

It's important to learn the fundamentals of business taxes from the start, so you can take advantage of every tax break owed you and keep as much of your startup's hard-earned money in your own pocket as possible.

Taxes scare many would-be entrepreneurs—for example, I talked to one recently who was afraid to hire contractors because of worries she would "get in trouble" with the IRS! Though our tax code is complicated, it's not inscrutable. Don't let fears about tax consequences keep you from starting your business.

The basics of business taxes aren't that hard to learn. You can do this.

If your business is complex—or you feel overwhelmed or unsure if you're taking all the deductions you should—hire a tax professional with small-business experience to help you. The Small Business and Self-Employed website of the IRS is also a great place to look if you have questions, as is the Starting & Managing a Business site of the Small Business Administration.

Here is a step-by-step guide to shrinking your tax burden:

GET SET UP RIGHT

The process of convincing the IRS that you run a real business begins with getting official paperwork filed with the IRS, as well as state and local authorities, that establishes your business name and structure. The SBA keeps a compendium of links to the appropriate state agency for each state.

To start, you'll want to register your business with your state and, in some locales, your city. You need to make sure no one else is already using the business name you have in mind. If your name is available, you want to register your business name so that no one else can start a business with the same name in your state later.

This is also the time to research your business type and make sure your city and state permit this type of business activity in the location you have planned. If you run afoul of local laws, you might find your business heavily taxed or even shut down.

For instance, my husband has experience selling cars and once had the idea to open his own car lot in our small town. This sounded like a great business idea to us, but Larry soon discovered it was out of the question.

Local codes specifically prohibited this business type unless the cars were housed in an enclosed building—no open-air car lots allowed. Our city fancies itself an upscale place and considers car lots cheesy. Since leasing an enclosed store big enough to create an indoor lot would be prohibitively expensive, the idea was a nonstarter. If he hadn't researched this question but had simply found an empty lot and started selling cars, he might have found himself in some costly legal trouble and likely would have had to close down.

State and local laws for business operation vary greatly. For example, a recent Institute for Justice study of business regulations in major cities found that in Philadelphia *no* businesses can be home-based—it is flat-out illegal. Some cities, including Miami, have stiff requirements for many industries and may require formal training and licensing. Make sure you are legally in the clear to start your business in your chosen location before you move forward.

Business Types

As you are registering your business, you will need to decide on a structure for your business. Here's a quick look at the choices and the tax and legal implications of each option:

Sole proprietor. This is the simplest, cheapest business form. As a sole proprietor, your business income is simply reported on your personal tax form's Schedule C. An important drawback of a sole proprietorship is that it does not shield your personal assets from legal action if someone sues your business. Translation: If your business runs into trouble, you could lose your house or any other personal valuables you possess.

Partnership. This is basically a sole proprietorship, only there are more owners. The business hasn't officially incorporated with the state, and the partners split the income by a formula they mutually decide upon. The partners then each pay tax on their portion of the business's revenue on their personal returns. As with a sole proprietorship, a partnership doesn't protect your personal assets if your business is sued.

Limited partnerships. This is a costly, complicated business type to set up and operate, and is generally not recommended for most small business owners. One owner must be designated the general partner, and others serve as limited partners. The general partner is responsible for day-to-day operations and is personally liable for business debts or claims—so you spend a lot to set up a limited partnership, but if you're the general partner, you could still lose your house in a lawsuit.

Limited liability company (LLC). Rules for LLCs were reformed in the 1990s to make it easier for even one-person businesses to incorporate as an LLC. As with a sole proprietorship, your business income is simply reported on your personal income taxes—it's known as a "pass-through entity" because your business income passes through to your personal tax form.

This is the simplest business structure for creating a legal wall between your personal assets and those of your company—it is called an LLC because it limits your liability to the assets of the business. Note, however, that an LLC does not protect you from every type of liability—if you personally harm someone, commit fraud, fail to deposit taxes withheld from employees' paychecks, or mingle your business and personal finances, your personal assets are still at risk.

S corporation. Incorporating as an S corporation is a more costly and complex process than forming an LLC but offers a tax-saving opportunity versus an LLC structure. This is because the owners of S corporations are paid a salary and can be paid bonuses. The company withholds taxes on these paychecks as it would for any employee, which means the company pays a portion of your employment tax, reducing your personal tax burden. The company then writes off its share of the employment tax as a business cost, reducing the business's taxable income. Unlike a C corporation, an S corporation's income is "passed through" to your personal tax form, the same as with an LLC. This structure shields your personal assets from being tapped to pay business debts.

C corporation. This structure is usually used only by large, established companies. This is because C corporations are subject to "double taxation"—the company pays tax on its revenue, and then you also pay tax on your share of profits on your personal income taxes.

Officials at your state agency may walk you through the process of incorporating your business. For outside help, you might hire an attorney who specializes in this area, or use websites such as MyCorporation.com to do it yourself. There are often fees of several hundred dollars to the state for registering as a corporation. On top of the registration fee, an attorney may charge $700–$1,000 or so to assist you in getting your paperwork straight. Discount websites will walk you through it for $50–$300, depending on the level of assistance you request.

The legal website Nolo.com is a good source of detailed information on each business type, its tax implications, and how to set up your business structure.

Business Versus Hobby

With your business officially registered and a business structure chosen, you've taken the first big step toward convincing the IRS that you have a legitimate business and not a hobby. This is an essential distinction.

If the IRS decides it's a hobby, the agency will disallow every dime of your business expenses. Then, you'll owe back taxes for all the years you claimed business expenses, along with penalties and interest, notes longtime CPA Paul Rafanello of Warwick, New York. Obviously, you want to avoid this at all costs!

One big way you can demonstrate to the IRS that you're running a real business is to make money. You will need to show a profit in at least two of five consecutive years, or you risk the IRS disqualifying all of the business expenses you've deducted in the previous years, says Rafanello.

For this reason, it's advisable to claim deductions of slightly less than your revenue total. It's more important to show a profit than to get more deductions, especially if you've taken a loss in a previous year or think you might need to declare one in the coming year.

Of course, it's also important that your business truly end up with a profit—so keep a close eye on how expenses are comparing to revenue. Use the tips in the preceding chapters to keep your expenses as low as possible.

Another way to look legit to the IRS is to keep careful track of all your business expenses. Virtually any activity you do in connection with your business is a potential write-off.

Business Deductions

The expenses you can deduct for your business vary from year to year as Congress frequently tinkers with the tax code—for instance, many new tax breaks were enacted to help business owners survive the economic downturn of 2008–2010. That said, here is a primer of basic types of expenses you should be sure to track:

Health-care costs. If your business offers health care to you, your family, and/or your employees, you may be able to deduct those premiums as well as any administrative costs. In addition, you may choose a healthcare plan that includes a health savings account (HSA). Individuals are permitted to deposit thousands annually (maximums change each year) with which to pay out-of-pocket medical expenses that your plan won't cover. Money deposited in these accounts is untaxed and reduces your gross income. For instance, I deposited more than $5,000 in an HSA in 2010. At an effective tax rate of nearly 30 percent, I saved more than $1,600 in taxes by tax-sheltering that income within the HSA account.

If your out-of-pocket health-care costs paid outside of an HSA exceed a certain percent of your income, you can take that as an additional health-care cost deduction.

When you start your business, you might still be on a former employer's plan through COBRA, the federal program that allows you to pay premiums and keep your existing health-care coverage. If so, these premium payments can be deducted dollar-for-dollar from the gross income of your business, says Rafanello.

Child care. If you are single and require child care in order to work, your child-care expenses are deductible. If you are married and you both work, you can likewise deduct child-care expenses. However, if you have a nonworking spouse but occasionally still hire sitters, you're out of luck.

To get this deduction, you'll need a tax identification or social security number for your sitter or child-care center. If you hire a nanny who works in your home, be warned that you may need to pay her as an employee.

Home office. If your business is run out of your home, you can take the home-office deduction. Rumors that taking this deduction is a sure-fire way to get audited by the IRS are unfounded, says Rafanello. However, the IRS likes to see a dedicated room of the house that isn't also used as a bedroom for that home office.

"It can't be the family room, with a TV in it and no door you can shut," Rafanello notes.

If you can show that your home is your business's primary base of operations, you will be able to deduct a portion of your mortgage interest, utilities, repairs, cleaning, and some other home costs as a business expense. Note that if you own your dwelling, you may owe a tax on the appreciation in value of that room when you sell.

Equipment. If you purchase equipment for your business, you can write that cost off. The timeframe varies from year to year, but generally you can write off a substantial sum—in 2011 it was $250,000—in the year you make the purchase. You can deduct any remainder as depreciation in the equipment's value over time, spread across the following five to seven years.

Operational costs. Expenses such as the cost of materials you need to create merchandise, or of merchandise you purchase from other manufacturers, advertising, interest on business or equipment-lease loans, office supplies, fees paid to professionals such as accountants or lawyers, rent, web hosting services, Internet, and utilities are all legitimate business deductions.

Employees and contractors. The IRS allows deductions both for payroll costs and for independent contractors you paid to perform services. But be warned that the IRS is very picky about how workers get classified and is on watch for contractors who are misclassified.

What's the difference? If you require workers to show up at your place of business for set hours, provide them with tools to do their job, and tell them how to do their work, the IRS will likely view these workers as employees. Contractors should be working independently at their own place of business, or setting their own hours if they are using your office. Contractors also work on a per-project fee basis rather than an hourly wage.

The IRS looks for evidence that your contractors are set up in business for themselves, says Rafanello.

"Do they have their own business card?" asks Rafanello. "Do they have a website? Do they have business insurance?" These basics of business ownership will signal to the IRS that someone is a legitimate contractor.

If you are hiring a relative such as one of your children to work in the business, there are some tax advantages to paying him or her as an employee. The child will not owe income tax on this pay unless it exceeds certain limits, and his or her pay also reduces your taxable gross income.

Meals and entertainment. If you take clients out to lunch or a movie while you try to win their business, a portion of this cost will be deductible. But take note that it's not a 100 percent deduction, and there are limits to how much you can claim here.

Travel. If you travel to trade shows, association meetings, or other events at which you are promoting your business, costs including airfare, mileage, hotel, meals, and entertainment are deductible. If you bring your family along, however, you cannot deduct any extra expenses such as a larger hotel room or your family's meals and entertainment costs.

Business vehicles and mileage. If you drive a vehicle of your own for your business, there are two different approaches you can take, notes Rafanello. If you only use the car for business, you can make it an asset of the business—but it's more difficult and costly to obtain insurance on a business vehicle. If it's a personal vehicle only partly used for business, you can take a deduction for the portion of time the car is used for business.

But in most cases, Rafanello says, it will be wiser for most new business owners to simply take the mileage deduction allowed by the IRS (the per-mile deduction figure changes annually). To qualify for the mileage deduction, though, you must keep a mileage log. The log should show the speedometer reading at the start of the year, and the readings for the beginning and end of each business trip you took as well as the final reading on the last day of the year. These figures allow you to calculate how many miles were driven for business.

Expense Tracking

To demonstrate to the IRS that you have a legitimate business, you'll want to set up a separate business checking account and pay all your business expenses through that account. If you use your personal checking account, it creates confusion about whether expenses are really business related and raises suspicion at the IRS that you have a hobby, not a business.

Create a system for capturing and tracking all your business expenses. Whether it's a shoebox you throw receipts in until year-end, a file folder, an Excel spreadsheet, or software such as Freshbooks or Quickbooks, find a system you can be consistent with and stick to it. If you're naturally disorganized, take advantage of low-cost tools such as Shoeboxed—which lets you scan and electronically store receipts—to make sure important receipts aren't lost.

The single best step you can take to shield your business from taxes is to set up your expense and income tracking system immediately—the moment you even think about starting a business—so that you document every cost and your business income from the very start.

Self-Employment Tax

When you were an employee, your employer deducted your share of employment tax from your paycheck, and you never really had to think about it. As a business owner, you will pay both portions, which usually doubles the amount you owe. Since you aren't receiving paychecks, it's your responsibility to set this money aside and have it ready to remit to the IRS at tax time.

In your first year of operation, estimate the tax bracket you expect to be in and simply set aside that portion of your income each month. After the first year, you will be asked to make quarterly estimated tax payments. It's not required, but you want to do this as it will spread the pain through the year rather than leaving you with a shocking tax bill all at once in April. You also may owe late fees or interest for not paying throughout the year.

Getting Your Taxes Done

At tax time, you have a decision to make about how to do your taxes. If your business is fairly straightforward, you may be able to use low-cost software such as TurboTax to walk you through the process.

But Rafanello advises that it's wise to hire a professional, especially when you've just started in business. Tax law changes constantly, and unless you want to become an expert in the tax code, consider at least consulting with a pro to make sure you're getting every possible deduction and your business is structured in the most tax-advantageous way.

What to Do if You Can't Pay

It can happen for a million different reasons: You didn't plan well. You made more than you imagined you would early in the year but then spent that cash during the year. You had some personal problems—a divorce, a major illness—that drained your cash.

Now, tax time arrives, and you don't have what you owe.

The key here is to not run and hide. If you fail to file your tax return, you are only increasing your costs. You will be fined for failing to file and will still owe penalties and interest on the taxes you should have paid. So file on time, and send in as much of your payment as you can.

At the same time, contact the IRS as soon as you know you can't pay. Especially if you have not come to the IRS before with this problem, agents may be receptive and willing to help you. After all, the agency would rather get some of what you owe than nothing.

The IRS has four options available to nonpayers:

1. **Noncollectible status.** If you believe your money problems are temporary, you can have your account placed in "currently not collectible" status. You'll need to prove your monthly income is equal or less than your essential expenses and that any assets such as home equity are inaccessible to you at this time.

2. **Short-term payoff.** If you will have the money to pay shortly, you can avoid fees by arranging to pay your taxes due in up to five monthly payments.

3. **Installment plan.** The IRS will create a payment agreement that gives you up to two years to pay the tab in monthly installments. Interest is compounded daily, and fees will rack up over time, so it's beneficial to pay it off as soon as you can. Interest rates change annually. You can even apply for an installment plan online.

4. Settlement offer. If you can show that it's unlikely you will ever be able to pay your income tax due, you can apply for an offer in compromise. The offer will propose settling your debt by paying a smaller amount than you owe, spread over monthly installments. In 2012, the IRS introduced the Fresh Start program, a reform designed to help more struggling taxpayers settle their outstanding tax bill. The new rules make it easier to get an offer in compromise accepted by the IRS.

Hopefully, your business will thrive, you'll track every possible deduction, and you'll remember to put away a portion of your income each month toward taxes. That will keep you from finding yourself in trouble at tax time.

Chapter 17

GETTING HELP

An entrepreneur's life can feel very lonely with the long hours you put in on your business. But it shouldn't be that way, particularly when you're starting. Instead, you should actively seek out experts and support organizations to advise and assist you. Having experienced mentors can save you a fortune in avoided missteps and poor execution as you seek to launch and grow your business.

Taking advantage of available free help is one of the best ways to save money in your business. Owners frequently pay big bucks to business consultants to come in and advise them on how to run their business better. But you may not have to if you take advantage of these resources.

The good news is that there is a lot of help available because the entire country is rooting for your business to succeed. No, seriously!

Small businesses are an important engine of economic growth for our country. The Small Business Administration's

Office of Advocacy reports that small businesses outperformed large ones in creating new jobs for 75 percent of all the years from 1992 through 2010.

Due to the important role of small businesses in the economic health of our nation, many support institutions have arisen to encourage and assist entrepreneurs in starting new businesses. These resources include:

- Government agencies and programs

- Business incubators

- Private and nonprofit business-assistance programs

This chapter provides you with an overview of the many resources available to you.

GOVERNMENT HELP

You can find business assistance at every level of government, but let's start with the biggest one, in Washington. The federal government's Small Business Administration focuses entirely on helping small businesses thrive. In recognition of the importance of this agency's work, in early 2012 President Barack Obama added the head of the SBA to his cabinet. The SBA offers online guides for every aspect of business operation, including:

- Market research

- Finding a mentor or counselor

- Startup step-by-step guides

- Registration and establishment of your business

- A primer in business law and regulations

- Marketing basics

- Lists of local resources

The SBA is also a major enabler of small-business funding through its SBA loan programs. The SBA does not directly make loans but offers guarantees to banks and sometimes creates financial incentives to encourage these lenders to make more small-business loans.

Other online resources include the SBA's community site as well as online courses and podcasts. The SBA has seven different types of regional business assistance offices across the country, each of which provides specialized help in the following particular areas:

SBA district offices. These regional offices oversee all SBA programs and are a good starting point to assess what help you need and where it might be available.

Small Business Development Centers (SBDCs). There is at least one SBDC in each state and sixty-three in all. The SBDCs are partnerships between the federal government and local colleges and universities. SBDCs coordinate educational programs for entrepreneurs in finance, marketing, manufacturing, business management, market research, engineering, and in resolving technical problems. The Association of Small Business Development Centers is a good resource for finding an SBDC near you. Often, SBDCs also house some of the programs listed just below, with dedicated staff for particular programs all located in the same office, or may partner with city or state business-assistance programs as well.

SCORE. This acronym stands for the Service Corps of Retired Executives. What's that? It's an association of seasoned, successful executives who have built and run their businesses for years and who voluntarily take time out of their retirement to share with you the wealth of their knowledge. If that sounds like an amazing free resource, it is. There are nearly 400 local SCORE chapters across the country. Through SCORE, you can connect with a mentor whom you can meet live, tap into local and online SCORE workshops, or even find an email mentor.

Women's Business Centers (WBCs). You can probably guess that WBCs focus on helping women entrepreneurs succeed. There are nearly 100 WBCs around the country, with the mission of "leveling the playing field" for women, helping them overcome obstacles and prejudice against women business owners. A related resource is the SBA's Office of Women's Business.

Veterans Business Outreach Centers. This program helps eligible veterans learn how to launch and run businesses. The program has sixteen different collaborating organizations that team to help vets create business plans, evaluate their business ideas, conduct feasibility studies, and receive mentoring help. In addition, the Department of Veterans Affairs in 2011 launched two new programs to assist vets in starting businesses: a business incubator in Wisconsin and a resource website, VetBiz.

US Export Assistance Centers. If your startup might import goods or sell to foreign markets, staff at these centers can help. The centers also have close relationships with the Export-Import Bank of the United States, the nation's primary funder of import-export loans. Export assistance has received renewed focus and additional resources since 2010, when President Obama announced the National Export Initiative, which aims to double US exports by the end of 2014.

Procurement Technical Assistance Centers (PTACs). Staff at these centers train business owners on how to become federal government contractors. PTACs help entrepreneurs get through the substantial required paperwork for government contractors, identify likely contracts to bid on, and learn to correctly estimate their bids. There are more than 100 PTACs nationwide. Given that the US Government spends roughly $320 billion annually on contracted goods and services, this is a market worth looking into for any entrepreneur.

State and Local Assistance. Many state and local governments are also active in helping to develop a thriving business climate in their locale. Some partner with the federal offices described above, while others run their own stand-alone programs. Inquire with your local chamber, city business-licensing office, or state business-development center to discover the available local resources to help your business grow.

BUSINESS INCUBATORS

Just as incubators help newly hatched chicks survive, business incubators are designed to nurture budding businesses until they're ready to go out on their own. While many company types have taken advantage of incubators, there is a strong emphasis on technology startups among the incubator programs.

Each incubator has its own approach to business assistance and support, but most offer a combination of free office space, mentoring, office supplies and services, and networking with local angel and venture capital funders. Many incubators are housed on college campuses and can offer some of the resources of their institution, including access to research labs. The application process varies—some college-based incubators take only current students, for instance—as does the length of time your startup might be allowed to stay in the incubator.

The incubator concept has been around since the 1950s, but the success of this model in launching new businesses in recent years has led to an explosion of incubator programs. The National Business Incubation Association now has more than 1,900 members internationally, with roughly three-quarters of those incubators based in the United States.

One of the most prestigious of this new crop is Silicon Valley's Y Combinator, founded in 2005. The Y Combinator model brings more than eighty startups to its complex twice a year for three months and gives each $18,000 in seed funding. More than 460 companies have been through the Y Combinator program, which culminates with a Demo Day, in which the startups pitch to a crowd of venture capitalists and angel investors. This basic model has been widely copied by many incubators.

Some incubators now specialize in a particular business type so that mentors can focus on an industry they know well. For instance, in early 2011 fashion designer Marc

Ecko's venture firm, Artists & Instigators, kicked off a program at the University of the Arts in Philadelphia that aimed to invest over $1 billion in 750 startups and create 20,000 student apprenticeships by 2016. And in Los Angeles, five-store chain Pitfire Artisan Pizza announced in mid-2012 that it was forming American Gonzo Food Corp., a restaurant incubator dedicated to developing new artisanal food brands.

Major corporations have also gotten into the incubator act, often assisting startups that might make good future acquisitions. Examples include the Procter & Gamble Co.'s P&G FutureWorks, which focuses on consumer-goods startups, and Samuel Adams' Brewing the American Dream, which works with aspiring craft brewers. The latter offered $1 million in microloans to startups around the country in 2012, along with mentoring and education.

Incubator Profile: TechStars

One of the largest and best-known incubator programs, TechStars, has locations in five cities and admits ten businesses at each location to its twice-yearly program. TechStars receives many applications and reports its acceptance rates are lower than Harvard's.

But the rewards for entrepreneurs who make it in are rich: Participants each receive $18,000 in cash and a $100,000 loan that's convertible to equity shares. Participating companies receive three months of in-house mentoring and assistance from more than seventy-five prominent venture capitalists who partner with the program.

TechStars has an impressive track record, too—of 126 startups the program shepherded from its founding in 2007 through mid-2012, roughly 10 percent had failed, while more than 7 percent were acquired, and the vast majority were still active. That compares favorably with general business failure rates—the SBA reports that about half of business startups fail within the first five years.

The TechStars model has won approval from Microsoft, which partnered with the incubator in 2012 to create a Microsoft Accelerator program.

Startup Case Study: Chirpify

If you're wondering how a stay in an incubator can save your business money, consider the experience of tech startup Chirpify based in Portland, Oregon. Founder Chris Teso had cofounded a previous digital services business, The Good, but when he had an idea for a product that would allow users to pay for items on Twitter, he split off to create Chirpify.

Teso says he applied to many incubators but found that few were interested in a one-person startup. Then he got an invitation from serial entrepreneur Greg Rau to bring his company to Rau's new business accelerator, Upstart Labs, in Portland. At the time, Teso says, Chirpify just had a prototype of its product, which needed refining to be scalable for Twitter's large audience. In an unusual model, Upstart provided what Teso estimates was $70,000 in free assistance, including use of the incubator's own in-house staff of software developers. Besides the financial savings, the expertise he got from Upstart's team was also invaluable in keeping development costs down.

"There was product advice I got that helped shape the final product, and some of that was making it even simpler,"

Teso says. "That, in effect, saved us even more money, since we didn't have to develop as many features."

This boost allowed Chirpify to launch its product in February 2012, making an immediate splash and landing $1.3 million in Series A funding from a top-flight group of investors including Voyager Capital, HootSuite CEO Ryan Holmes, and angel-funding group TiE Oregon Angels, among others. Chirpify had grown to a team of seven by mid-2012.

Government Support for Incubators

The federal government is getting more involved in incubators, too. In early 2011, President Obama announced the Startup America Partnership. Chaired by AOL founder Steve Case, this initiative brings the White House together with major corporations to foster startups, support business incubators around the country, and encourage business innovation. As part of the kickoff, IBM pledged to spend $150 million on business-mentoring programs, and Intel committed $200 million toward venture funding of startups. By 2012, the partnership had established two dozen incubator sites.

Federal Jobs Bill money also is flowing to incubators: For instance, the state incubator Connecticut Innovations, which runs a TechStars-affiliated program, received $1 million in federal funding to support its incubator in 2012.

As more and more success stories arise from incubators, this model for fostering business growth is making its way into the halls of government, too. For instance, a new course in entrepreneurship at Stanford University, the Lean LaunchPad, has inspired the National Science Foundation to start its own incubator program. The NSF's

Innovation-Corps, or I-Corps, launched in mid-2011 as a public-private partnership designed to aid scientists in developing their ideas and inventions more readily into viable businesses.

Initially, I-Corps pledged to support up to 100 startups a year at $50,000 per project. The six-month program includes mentoring, feasibility studies, and competitive research to help determine the viability of new innovations in the commercial marketplace.

State and city officials are also hosting incubator programs in hopes of improving the economic scene in their own regions. After all, every city would like to see a new Apple or Google birthed within their borders so the municipality could reap the sales-tax bonanza.

One of the largest state incubator programs is MassChallenge, a business accelerator sponsored by the state of Massachusetts, Verizon, Microsoft, and many charitable foundations. The program accepts startups of all types and locales, and assists a large number of entrepreneurs.

Three hundred semifinalists receive feedback on their business ideas annually from a judging panel, and 125 finalists take part in MassChallenge's three-month mentoring program, which includes free office space, access to funders, and media exposure. At the conclusion of each session, more than $1 million in cash is awarded to participants plus over $4 million in related technical support.

Quickie Incubators or "Unconferences"
While traditional incubators usually house startups for several months or longer, there is also a recent movement to

much shorter, loosely organized business conclaves that aim to help startups take big leaps forward in just a weekend by collaborating with mentors and each other. A notable example is BarCamp, a movement of user-generated events that started in 2005. Since then, hundreds of BarCamps have been held throughout the world. A recent BarCamp event in Nashville, Tennessee, was described as "equal parts networking, knowledge-building and fun."

BarCamp programs are loosely organized over the Internet by the participants. The content of each camp is defined by the attendees, who are all expected to present or facilitate a session. Many more people often participate in BarCamps via the Internet and through social media as sessions are in progress. Common BarCamp themes include web application building, open-source technologies and data formats, and social media.

The BarCamp model has been widely copied in other industries, and themed events that have resulted include EcoCamp (for ecology-focused startups) and PodCamp (for podcasters and other startups in new media). After a BarCamp or similar event, participants often continue collaborating virtually through online collaboration tools such as Google Groups.

NONPROFIT ASSISTANCE PROGRAMS

Besides government and corporate assistance, there are also substantial resources for startup owners in the nonprofit sector. Many nonprofits are focused entirely on fostering entrepreneurship. A good starting point for finding local entrepreneurship organizations that might help you is the web portal US SourceLink, which lists resources from more than 5,000 entrepreneurial support organizations.

The world's largest foundation dedicated to entrepreneurship is the Ewing Marion Kauffman Foundation in Kansas City, Missouri. Kauffman was a farm-raised entrepreneur who founded pharmaceutical giant Marion Laboratories. Kauffman is one of the organizers of Global Entrepreneurship Week, a weeklong event designed to foster entrepreneurship in youth that takes place at hundreds of sites.

Among Kauffman's many resources to assist startups is the portal Will It Be You, which outlines Kauffman programs that offer learning and mentorship, as well as those of affiliate organizations. Other Kauffman resources include FastTrac, an umbrella for online and in-person entrepreneurship training programs, and the Urban Enterprise Partnership, which assists urban and minority entrepreneurs in four economically distressed regions.

Nonprofit Organization Profile: Washington Community Alliance for Self-Help (CASH)

Seattle-based Washington CASH was founded in 1995 after its founder, longtime Expeditors International CEO Peter Rose, was inspired by India's microlending powerhouse the Grameen Bank. Washington CASH's program focuses on low-income entrepreneurs, providing an eight-week training course, follow-up support, and access to capital at four program sites around the Seattle area.

The program makes a dramatic difference for the business owners who participate. Surveys taken eighteen months after participation in Washington CASH found that nearly one-quarter of the owners had hired an employee. The median income increase was 44 percent for those who came to the program with an established small business.

CASE STUDY: RUSH SECURITY

Augie Lujan knew he wanted to start his own business when he got out of the military in 2003, but it took a few years for his dream to gain traction. In 2009, he heard about Washington CASH and went to an initial meeting. At the time, he had just registered a business name for his planned security firm—Rush Security—but wasn't sure how to move forward to get the business off the ground. He was accepted into the program and conducted a feasibility study during the eight-week training.

This research showed Lujan what existing security companies in his region of Kitsap County, Washington, offered and what they charged. He identified a market opportunity— none of the other companies offered armed security. This insight motivated Lujan to obtain the needed licensing to offer this specialized service, which is needed for situations such as late-night ATM repairs and protecting the cashbox at large nonprofit events.

"Now, we get some bigger national contracts, just because we are the only business here with armed security guards," he says.

One SBA guest speaker who spoke to his Washington CASH class saved Lujan a bundle. Governments are major customers for outsourced security work, and Lujan was considering paying a service upwards of $10,000 for help in locating and obtaining government contracts. The SBA official warned Lujan away from this idea, showing him where free and low-cost resources were available to help him with the process instead.

In its third year, Bremerton-based Rush Security saw $140,000 in revenue. Lujan has twenty mostly part-time employees. He says that beyond the initial training, he found ongoing biweekly support meetings that held him accountable for meeting his goals. These proved to be an essential support as he started and grew the business.

"I don't know if the business would have lasted without the support that was there at Washington CASH," he says.

To sum up, these government, incubator, and nonprofit resources exist to help you. Advice and support from experienced business owners is a proven way to save your business money and increase its odds of success. Investigate the assistance available in your area—and take advantage of it.

Chapter 18

RESOURCES

These resource links are listed by chapter and in the order in which they appeared within that chapter. In the case of resources that appear more than once, the resource is listed the first time it appeared.

Chapter 1 – Market Research

SBA statistics on business survival rates: www.sba.gov/sites/default/files/sbfaq/pdf

PR Newswire: www.prnewswire.com/

PRWeb: www.prweb.com/

Technomic: www.technomic.com/

Slideshare: www.slideshare.net/

Directions on Microsoft: www.directionsonmicrosoft.com/

Tradepub.com: www.tradepub.com/

Chain Store Guide: www.chainstoreguide.com/

Hoovers: www.hoovers.com/

SurveyMonkey: www.surveymonkey.com/

Time banks: http://timebanks.org/

Barter exchanges: www.gigafree.com/barter.html

Junior Achievement: www.ja.org/

Future Business Leaders of America: www.fbla-pbl.org/

Steven Blank: http://steveblank.com/books-for-startups/

Chapter 2 – Business Plan

Edgar: www.sec.gov/edgar.shtml

SBA guide to writing a business plan: www.sba.gov/ category/navigation-structure/starting-managing-business/starting-business/how-write-business-plan

Free business plan templates: www.bplans.com/

Chapter 3 – Training

US Department of Labor's Office of Apprenticeship: www.doleta.gov/oa/employer.cfm

Links to state apprenticeship offices: www.doleta.gov/oa/ stateoffices.cfm

America's Swimming Pool Co.: http://americasswim-mingpoolcompany.com/

Association for Career and Technical Education: www .acteonline.org/

US Department of Education Accreditation: http://ope .ed.gov/accreditation/

The Learning Annex: www.learningannex.com/

Lynda Online Tutorials: www.lynda.com/

W3Schools: http://www.w3schools.com/

SBA resources on business operations: www.sba.gov/ category/navigation-structure/starting-managing-business/starting-business

Chapter 4 – E-Commerce

AppSumo: www.appsumo.com/

Astonish Inc.: http://astonishinc.com/

VStore: www.vstore.ca/

Google Keyword Analytics tool: www.googlekeywordtool
.com/

Keyword Spy: www.keywordspy.com

SEMRush: www.semrush.com

SEOMoz: www.seomoz.org/

Scribe SEO: http://scribeseo.com/

Apache Open Office: www.openoffice.org/

Libre Office: www.libreoffice.org/download/

Google Docs: https://docs.google.com/#home

Gmail: mail.google.com/

Mailchimp: http://mailchimp.com/f/

Grasshopper: http://grasshopper.com/

OpenVBX: http://openvbx.org/

Google Calendar: www.google.com/calendar/

SimpleInvoices: www.simpleinvoices.org/

Freshbooks: www.freshbooks.com/

SohoOS: www.sohoos.com/welcome/

Evernote: http://evernote.com

FreeGraphics.org: www.freegraphics.org/

Flickr Creative Commons: www.flickr.com/
creativecommons/

MorgueFile: www.morguefile.com/

Free Digital Photos: www.freedigitalphotos.net/

Jing: www.techsmith.com/jing.html

GitHub: https://github.com/

MyCorporation: www.mycorporation.com/

Google AdSense: www.google.com/adsense/
The NieNie Dialogues: http://nieniedialogues.com/

Chapter 5 – Sales

Brad's Raw Chips: www.bradsrawchips.com/
Salesforce: www.salesforce.com/
Simplicity Consulting: http://simplicityconsultinginc
.com/
RainToday case study on Simplicity: www.raintoday.
com/library/case-studies/relationship-based-sales-
model-grows-consulting-firm-from-300k-to-115m-in-
3-years/

Chapter 6 – Marketing

LinkedIn Social Media Marketing group: www.linkedin.
com/groups/Social-Media-Marketing-66325
VistaPrint: www.vistaprint.com/
PRLog: www.prlog.org/
Toastmasters: www.toastmasters.org/
eZine Articles: http://ezinearticles.com
Answers.com: www.answers.com
HootSuite: http://hootsuite.com/
Tweetdeck: www.tweetdeck.com/
Anymeeting: www.anymeeting.com/
Bing Business Portal: www.bing.com/businessportal/
Yahoo! Local: http://local.yahoo.com/
Shoes of Prey: www.shoesofprey.com/
Blair Fowler/JuicyStar07: www.youtube.com/user/
juicystar07
Google Analytics: www.google.com/analytics/

Chapter 7 – Collaboration and Partnerships

Girls Night Out: http://downtownolympia.com/about/girlsnightout/

Dinner in White: http://paris.untappedcities.com/2010/06/13/diner-en-blanc-white-party/

Naked Marketing: http://nakedmarketingmanifesto.com/nm/

Chapter 8 – Advertising

EZTexting: www.eztexting.com

Moto Message: www.motomessage.com/

Appmakr: www.appmakr.com/

Chapter 9 – Facilities

Skillet Street Food: http://skilletstreetfood.com/

Extreme ReTrailers: www.extremeretrailers.com/

Coworking: http://coworking.com/

The Hub: www.the-hub.net/network

NextSpace: http://nextspace.us/

Gordon Brothers Group: www.gordonbrothers.com/

Chapter 10 – Operations

Skype: www.skype.com/intl/en-us/home

Keku: www.keku.com/

Green Pro Systems: www.greenprosystems.com/

Foundation for Responsible Technology: www.foundationforresponsibletechnology.org/

Chapter 11 – Purchasing

Liquidation.com: www.liquidation.com/

CloseoutsWorld: www.closeoutsworld.com/

Independent Pharmacy Buying Group: www.ipbg.biz/pages/1/index.htm

Independent Stationers: www.independentstationers.coop/

MEGA Group: www.megagroupusa.com/

Alibaba: www.alibaba.com/

Better World Books: http://www.betterworldbooks.com/

Chapter 12 – Transportation and Shipping

Pactiv: www.pactiv.com/index.aspx

Packsize: www.packsize.com/

123Loadboard: www.123loadboard.com/backhaul-freight/

Load Authority: www.loadauthority.com/

Shiply: www.shiply.com/

Chapter 13 – Labor

Department of Labor unpaid internship rules: www.dol.gov/whd/regs/compliance/whdfs71.htm

Fair Labor Standards Act: www.dol.gov/compliance/laws/comp-flsa.htm

99 Designs: https://99designs.com/

Amazon Mechanical Turk: www.mturk.com/mturk/welcome

Craigslist: www.craigslist.org/about/sites

Elance: www.elance.com

FlexJobs: www.flexjobs.com/

Freelancer: www.freelancer.com/

GetaCoder: www.getacoder.com/

Guru.com: www.guru.com

oDesk: www.odesk.com/

People Per Hour: www.peopleperhour.com/
Paleo Plan: www.paleoplan.com/
Monster.com: www.monster.com/

Chapter 14 – Financing

SBIR/SBTT program: www.sbir.gov/about/about-sbir
InvestMaryland: www.gov.state.md.us/pressreleases/
100601.asp
National Venture Capital Association statistics: www
.nvca.org/index.php?Itemid = 147&id = 119&
option = com_content&view = article
JOBS Act: http://majorityleader.gov/uploadedfiles/
JOBSACTOnePager.pdf
MicroVentures: www.microventures.com/
CircleUp: https://circleup.com/
AngelList: https://angel.co/
Aspen Institute study of microlending: http://fieldus.org/
Publications/FY2010CensusHighlightsNEW.pdf
Grameen Bank: www.grameen.com/
Accion USA: www.accionusa.org/
Prosper.com: www.prosper.com/
LendingClub: www.lendingclub.com/
KickStarter: www.kickstarter.com/
ZimpleMoney: www.zimplemoney.com/

Chapter 15 – Cash Flow

Equifax: www.equifax.com/home/en_us
Experian: www.experian.com/
TransUnion: www.transunion.com/

Chapter 16 – Taxes

IRS Small Business and Self-Employed website: www.irs
.gov/businesses/small/index.html

SBA: Starting and Managing a Business: www.sba.gov/
category/navigation-structure/starting-managing-
business

SBA list of state agencies: www.sba.gov/content/search-
business-licenses-and-permits

Institute for Justice study of barriers to entrepreneurship:
http://ij.org/city-studies-on-barriers-to-entrepreneurship

Nolo.com: www.nolo.com/

Paul Rafanello, CPA: www.prcpa.biz

Quickbooks: http://quickbooks.intuit.com/

Shoeboxed: www.shoeboxed.com/

TurboTax: http://turbotax.intuit.com/

IRS tax payment installment plan application: www.irs
.gov/individuals/article/0,,id = 149373,00.html

IRS Fresh Start program: http://www.irs.gov/uac/
Newsroom/IRS-Fresh-Start-Program-Helps-Taxpayers-
Who-Owe-the-IRS

Chapter 17 – Getting Help

SBA Office of Advocacy study of small business job
creation: www.sba.gov/advocacy/809/130751

SBA community site: www.sba.gov/community

SBA online training: www.sba.gov/content/starting-
business

SBA offices: www.sba.gov/about-offices-list/2

SBDCs: www.sba.gov/content/small-business-development-
centers-sbdcs

Association of Small Business Development Centers: www.asbdc-us.org/

SCORE: www.score.org/

Women's Business Centers: www.sba.gov/about-offices-content/1/2895/resources/13729

SBA Office of Women's Business: www.sba.gov/about-offices-content/1/2895

Veterans Business Outreach Centers: www.sba.gov/content/veterans-business-outreach-centers

VetBiz: www.vetbiz.gov/

US Export Assistance Centers: www.sba.gov/content/us-export-assistance-centers

National Export Initiative: http://trade.gov/nei/

Procurement Technical Assistance Centers: www.sba.gov/content/procurement-technical-assistance-centers-ptacs

National Business Incubation Association: www.nbia.org/

Y Combinator: http://ycombinator.com/

Artists & Instigators: www.artistsandinstigators.com/

P&G FutureWorks: http://futureworks.pg.com/

Samuel Adams' Brewing the American Dream: http://btad.samueladams.com/Default.aspx?TabID = 105

TechStars: www.techstars.com/program/

SBA report on business failure rates: www.sba.gov/sites/default/files/sbfaq.pdf

Microsoft accelerator: www.microsoft.com/bizspark/kinectaccelerator/

Chirpify: http://chirpify.com/

Upstart Labs: www.upstartlabs.com/

Startup America Partnership: www.s.co/

I-Corps: www.nsf.gov/news/news_summ.jsp?cntn_id = 12 1225&org = NSF&from = new

MassChallenge: http://masschallenge.org

BarCamp: http://barcamp.org/

US SourceLink: www.ussourcelink.com/

Ewing Marion Kauffman Foundation: www.kauffman .org/

Global Entrepreneurship Week: www.kauffman.org/ uploadedFiles/FactSheet/GEWFactSheet032709.pdf

Will It Be You: www.willitbeyou.com/

FastTrac: http://fasttrac.org/

Urban Enterprise Partnership: www.uepkauffman.org/

Washington CASH: http://washingtoncash.org/

Rush Security: www.rushsecurity.net/

Conclusion

Is your head bursting with ideas on how you can save money in your business? I certainly hope so!

If the tips in this book help you save money in your startup, I'd love to hear from you about it. I'd also like to hear if you come across any additional money saving resources that we might add to future editions of this book.

You can send me an email at carol@caroltice.com or learn more about me at www.caroltice.com. To download the companion workbook to *Pocket Small Business Owner's Guide to Starting Your Business on a Shoestring*, please visit Shoestringstartupguide.com/download.

Index